Myron A Hunt

How to Grow Cut Flowers

A practical treatise on the cultivation of the rose, carnation, chrysanthemum, voilet, and other winter flowering plants

Myron A Hunt

How to Grow Cut Flowers

A practical treatise on the cultivation of the rose, carnation, chrysanthemum, voilet, and other winter flowering plants

ISBN/EAN: 9783337256395

Printed in Europe, USA, Canada, Australia, Japan

Cover: Foto ©Lupo / pixelio.de

More available books at **www.hansebooks.com**

How to Grow Cut Flowers.

A PRACTICAL TREATISE

ON THE CULTIVATION OF THE ROSE,
CARNATION, CHRYSANTHEMUM, VIOLET, AND OTHER
WINTER FLOWERING PLANTS.

ALSO

GREENHOUSE CONSTRUCTION.

ILLUSTRATED.

A BOOK FOR THE FLORIST AND AMATEUR.

BY

M. A. HUNT.

PUBLISHED BY THE AUTHOR.
1893.

Entered according to Act of Congress, in the year 1893, by
M. A. HUNT,
In the Office of the Librarian of Congress, at Washington

PRESS OF MOORE & LANGEN,
TERRE HAUTE.

LIBRARY

Department of Floriculture *and* Ornamental Horticulture

NEW YORK STATE COLLEGE
of AGRICULTURE

at CORNELL UNIVERSITY
ITHACA, N.Y.

CONTENTS.

		PAGE
PREFACE		i-iii
CHAPTER.—I.	Greenhouse Construction	1-17
II.	Ventilation—How Constructed	18-22
III.	The Short Span to the South	23-28
IV.	Greenhouse Heating	29-30
V.	Hot Water Heating	31-34
VI.	The Down-Hill System	35-36
VII.	Hot Water under Pressure	37-38
VIII.	Heating by Steam	39-43
IX.	Overhead Heating	44
X.	Roses—Their Cultivation	45-46
XI.	Soil	47-49
XII.	Stock for Planting	50-56
XIII.	The Renewal of Rose Plants	57-58
XIV.	Roses in Summer	59-61
XV.	Depth of Soil for Planting	62-63
XVI.	Planting	63-65
XVII.	Staking and Tying	66-71
XVIII.	Mulching	72-73
XIX.	Watering	74-76
XX.	Ventilation	78-80
XXI.	Temperature of Water	81-83
XXII.	Shading	84-85
XXIII.	The Cutting of Buds	86-89
XXIV.	Grading and Packing	90
XXV.	The Preservation of Flowers	91-93
XXVI.	Insect Enemies	94-107
XXVII.	Insect Exterminators	108-118
XXVIII.	Diseases of the Rose	119-126
XXIX.	Forcing Varieties—Cultural Notes	127-140
XXX.	The Forcing of Hybrids	141-147
XXXI.	Florists' Green	148-152
XXXII.	The Carnation	153-167
XXXIII.	Diseases of the Carnation	168-180
XXXIV.	Chrysanthemums	181-187
XXXV.	Violets	188-194
XXXVI.	Mignonette	195-197
XXXVII.	The Forcing of Bulbs	198-205
XXXVIII.	Orchids	206-208
XXXIX.	Miscellaneous Topics	209-228

ILLUSTRATIONS.

	PAGE
Anthracnose of Carnation	173
Benching	9–11
Black Spot	124–125
Bacterial Disease of Carnation	175
Club Root	103
Down-Hill System of laying Water-pipes	32
End of Sash Bar—How Made	14
Evaporating Pan	109
Form of Gutter where Houses Join	7
Forcing House for Lily of the Valley	201
Gauge for setting Bars	16
Gutter for Outside Wall	6
How to Join Gutters	5
Header used at foot of Ventilator	15
How to fill in between the foot of the Bars	16
Method of Laying Hot Water Pipes	32
Movable Wire Frame for Staking	69
New Method of Building	28
Pot Racks	212
Ridge—how joined	13
Red Spider	94
Rose Bug and Larva	96–97
Rust on Carnation leaf	169
Roof—how supported	12
Ridge—how supported	13
Side Ventilation	20
Spot on Carnations	172
The First American Greenhouse	Frontispiece
Three-Fourths Span House	10
The Short Span to the South	24–26
Thrip	93
Vaporizing Tank and Pipes	111–112
Violet House	190
Violet Root Galls	193
Wire Support for Carnations	159
Zinc Joint	17

INDEX.

	PAGE
Adiantums, to grow	150
American Beauty, cuttings for	54
Treatment of	136
Ammonia, to use	163, 217, 205
Asparagus Plumosa	152
Black spot, remedy for	127
Bone Meal, value of	215
Boilers, care of	224
Bulbs, how forced	198
Calla Lilly, to grow	205
Carnations, average night temperature	161
Cut worms on	166
Cuttings, when made	157, 179, 180
Early planting	157
Fungoid diseases of	169, 173
Remedies for	174, 177
Fertilizers for	163, 164
Grading the flowers	168
Improvements in	153
Insects injurious to	165, 166
Rust on	169
To prevent	171
Soil for	163
Supporting, how performed	159, 160
Vitality lost	155
When to house	158
When to syringe	165
Chrysanthemums, black apis to kill	187
Crops to succeed them	182
Cuttings, when made	182, 184
Distance to plant	184
Grown in Sprays	182
To single flowers	183
Grown in pots	185
New disease of	186
Soil for	183
Varieties for cut flowers	186

INDEX.

	PAGE
Cement, use of	222
C. Mermet, temperature for	131
Cleanliness	209
Club root, to prevent	105, 214
Coal tar, its use	219
Crude oil	221
Cuttings, wood for	51
Cut worms	166, 167
Disbudding carnations	165
Chrysanthemums	185
Roses	223
Distillery manure, value of	215
Eel worms, to prevent	105
Fertilizers	215
Florists' Green	146
Freezias	200
Fungus in cutting bed, cure for	177
Fumigating	117
Green Fly, to kill	108, 117
Greenhouse Construction	1
Benches, how made	9, 11, 12
Butted glass	17
Gutters, how to join	5
How to attach roof to gutter	16
Houses for summer growing	223
Length of a house	4
Lumber, kind to use	3, 4, 8, 9
New style of house	28
Outside wall, to cover	8
Painting	14, 17
Purlin, what made of	13
Ridge, how made	9
Roof, to raise	15
Size of glass	17
Solid bench, new method	10
Support of ridges	13
Short span to the south	23, 26
Ventilation	18, 19
In wall	20, 21
Greenhouse Heating	29
Boiler, kind to use	89
Fuel to use	30
Heating by steam	30

INDEX.

	PAGE
Greenhouse Heating.—	
Hot water heating	13
Under pressure	37, 38
Pipes to lay	33, 35
Overhead heating	44
The down hill system	36
The best system of heating	42, 43
Steam boiler, to set	40
Pipes, size of	41
Number of	42
To lay	42
Harrisii, how forced	202
How to Scald a House	210
Horn Shavings	219
Hops, use of	164
How to Repair a Brick Fire Box	226
Hot Water, to heat with	31
Insect Exterminators	108, 118
Lily of the Valley, house for	201
Forcing of	202
Lilium Candidum	204
Liquid Manure	218
Leaking Pipes, to stop	227
Madam Hoste, treatment	140
Meteor, temperature for	130
Mortar for Fire Brick, to make	226
Miscellaneous topics	209
Mildew, how to prevent	120, 123
Mignonette, butterfly to kill	196
Disease, remedy for	197
House, how constructed	196
Seed, selection of	195
When sown	196
Temperature for	197
Narcissus	198
Nitrate of Soda	217
Niphetos, budded on	61
Orchids	206
Best varieties to grow	208
Overhead Heating	44
Papa Gontier, treatment of	134
Pot Racks	212
Preparation of Soil	213
Roses	45, 46

Roses.   PAGE
  American Beauty 54, 136
  A cellar for 92, 93
  Black Spot on 124, 126
  Buds, Grading and Packing 90
      How to cut 88, 89
      How to preserve 91
  Catharine Mermet 131
  Club Root 102
      To prevent 105, 106
  Cultural Notes on 125, 140
  Depth of soil to plant in . . 62
  Diseases of 119
  Forcing varieties of 127
  Hybrids, forcing of 141, 147
  Impaired vitality 55, 56, 222
  La France, culture of 135
  Madam Cusin 140
  Madam Hoste 140
  Madam P. Guillott . . . 137
  Madam Watteville . . . 138
  Meteor 130
  Mealy Bug, to kill . . . 99
  Mildew, to prevent . . . 119
  Mulching of 72, 73
  Movable frame for . . . 70, 71
  New varieties . . . 141
  Niphetos . . . 133
  Papa Gontier . . . 134
  Perle des Jardins . . . 128
  Planting, when and how . . . 63
  Propagating from blind wood . . . 51, 52
  Resting of . . . 54
  Renewal of . . . 57
  Red Spider . . . 94, 95
  Solid beds for . . . 62
  Shading of . . . 84, 85
  Souv de Wootton . . . 139
  Staking and tying . . . 66
  Summer growing of . . . 59, 60
      Varieties for 61
  Thrip . . . 96
  The Bride 133
  The Leaf Roller 98

INDEX.

	PAGE
Roses.—	
The Rose Bug	. 96, 97
Two-eyed cottings	. 53
Ventilating	. 77, 80
Watering	. 74, 76
Water, temperature of	81
White Grub in	. 101
Wire stakes, cost of	. 72
W. F. Bennett	. 139
Roman Hyacinths	. 198
Salt, its use	. 211
Sod, when to cut	. 214
Soil for certain varieties	. . 47, 50
How to prepare	. 213, 214
Used the second year	. . 220
Steam, to heat with	. 89
Smilax, to destroy worms on	. 149, 167
Stock for planting	50
Tobacco extract	. 110
Trough for evaporating	. 109
Tulips, forcing of	. 198
Vaporizing tobacco	. 111
Vitality lost how restored	. . 223
Violet, club root in	. . 193
Diseases of	. 192, 195
Fungus on	. . . 194
House, how to build	. . 190
How to plant	. 189
Wood ashes	. . 216
White grub	. 101, 215

PREFACE.

Cut flowers have become a great article of commerce, and the demand for them increases with each passing year. How to grow them to a profit is the great question with the professional florist. How to grow them successfully, and thus derive a maximum of pleasure from the outlay, is what most interests the amateur. An answer to these questions is what the author has sought to give in these pages. Notwithstanding this industry represents millions of capital, and gives employment to many thousands of people, there exists, as yet, no book which gives the seeker after information, any knowledge concerning this great and constantly increasing business. Nor is there any defined process by which the amateur devoid of professional training, who desires to grow for his own pleasure, may do so with any reasonable hope of success.

To be sure, trade journals and amateur magazines have been established within a few years, in which valuable experiences have appeared from time to time, but scarcely a decade has passed since a majority of the writers were themselves novices, groping in the dark as many a grower is obliged to do to-day. A few wide awake young men are to be found each year, giving time with some of the best growers. If bright and quick to observe, they are in a few years fitted either to conduct business for themselves, or for others. To the majority, this method of study is not practicable, and there seems to be no way of mastering the business, but by stumbling on from year to year, making mistakes and undertaking experiments so costly in themselves, that when the lesson derived from them is learned, one finds himself in the possession of an experience, purchased at the cost of valuable time, and oftentimes with a balance on the wrong side of the ledger.

Nor are those who are thus struggling along, traveling a new road; it is a well beaten path, and many of us have pursued it so long, the years in the meantime have slipped away and more gray hairs than riches are left in their train. We have had the experience, but at what a cost?

I well remember, when a young man full of enthusiasm and at just that time of life when one knows more than any who have gone before, or who will ever come after him, having made an experiment contrary to the advice of those older than myself, and having had the mortification of seeing it fail, trying to draw consolation from the fact that I had the experience left, how well I remember my father's reply: "My son, purchased wit is good if not bought too dear." Well—I have been buying just such wit as that all my life, and it is with a view to assist those who are just entering the road over which I have traveled, that I have undertaken to chronicle the result of experiences that have come to me with the passing years.

Could I have had access to the contents of this book fifteen years ago, no price within the limit of my means would have been too great for it, as it would have saved me thousands of dollars, and would undoubtedly have added some years to a life that has seen much of the "wear and tear" that comes from an uphill fight with circumstances.

In the compiling of this volume no claim is made to infallibility. Some of the deductions may not be in accord with the experience of others, but the facts have been stated as found by the author. It is a plain story, the result of a life of both experience and observation.

To the professors in our experimental stations we are indebted for much of the light already shed upon the diseases incident to plant life. To them, and all others whose opinions have been quoted in these pages, the author desires to acknowladge his personal obligations.

M. A. HUNT.

TERRE HAUTE, January, 1893.

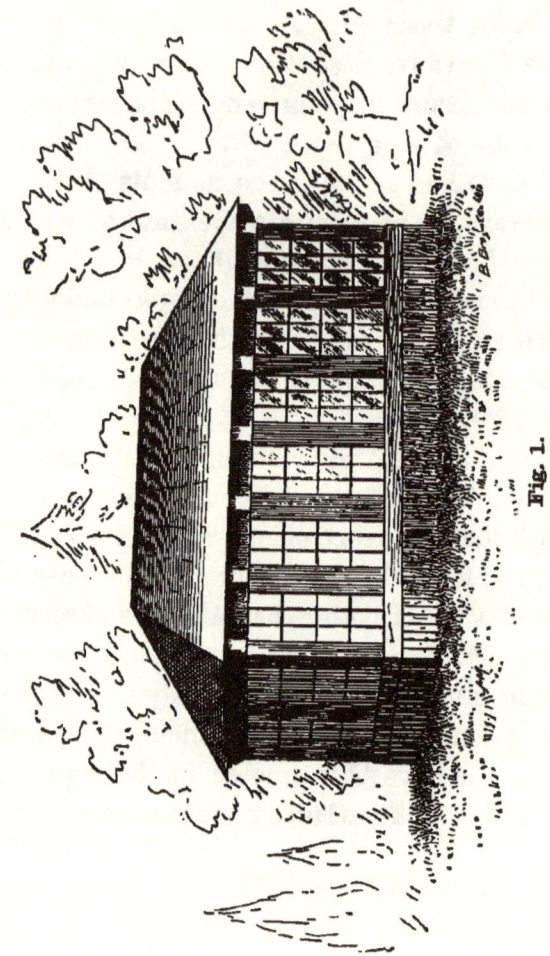

Fig. 1.

THE FIRST AMERICAN GREENHOUSE.

CHAPTER I.
GREENHOUSE CONSTRUCTION.

The first question which occurs to the thoughtful man, is, how and where shall I build? If you are already located in some town or city, and desire to use your improvements for the supply of your own retail trade, draw your plans with that end in view, as the buildings will need to be adapted to the space you have to fill as well as to the miscellaneous character of the stock you wish to grow. When making your plan, look forward to any possible future need. Let it be carefully studied out in such a way that it may be easily added to from year to year as your needs demand, and still, when a complete whole, all may come within your original draft.

We find many places, oftentimes of considerable size, so inconvenient and built at such varying angles as to render it almost necessary for a stranger to have the services of a guide, in order to find his way out after having once entered the intricate collection. Remembrances such as these bring a sigh of relief when one enters a well ordered, well kept range of houses. If you are at a loss how to plan your space yourself, obtain the assistance of some man of experience in whose good judgment you have confidence, but unless you want an elaborate office front, avoid the professional architect, for as a rule architects have had no experience in this class of building, and their drawings are on too expensive a scale to be followed.

If you are building for commercial purposes, or for the growth of cut flowers merely, for your own use, let your location be such as will embrace as many as possible of the following requirements. These are placed in the order, as it seems to me, of their importance. Adaptability of soil, pure fresh air and sheltered location, nearness of fuel, proximity to your intended market. Of soils and fuel I shall have occasion to speak under their separate heads.

In locating where land is reasonable in price so that all that is needed may be obtained, it is well to seek some natural shelter from the prevailing winds, and in the absence of such shelter protect your buildings by artificial means, such as the planting of evergreen trees. Select such trees as will grow to a good height, and when strong winds come you will find it a great protection. Having settled these preliminaries as best you can, decide how well you wish to build, but do not make the mistake of trying to make money go too far; it is better to build one house fairly well than to build two so cheaply that their term of service will be short.

If you are able to build of iron you will find firms who make the building of such houses a specialty. To the man of moderate means, however, I believe there is a happy medium between these costly iron structures and the cheap, short-lived buildings we so often meet, in the construction of which there is no economy.

If you are in a location where lumber is cheap, and where all that is needed in building can be readily obtained, it will of course be to your interest to patronize your home market; but even in this case, it will doubtless save you time and money to order your roof of some person or firm making a specialty of this class of work, whose advertisements may be found in the trade journals. In regard to the kind of lumber to use, the part just referred to is at the present time mostly made of cypress, and is, probably, as cheap and durable as any. At the present writing, I am repairing houses built ten years since, the roofing of which was white pine, and with few exceptions, the indications would seem to be that the sash bars are good for ten years more. Whatever kind of wood you select for the roof, gutters and posts, discard every piece showing any sap, as it will soon decay and destroy the whole or render repairs necessary at an early date. The desirability of building houses three-fourths span with a south exposure, has been unquestioned by all the best growers. The general impression seems to be no other pitch can give as good results in December and January, the months when cut flowers pay the best. If properly constructed as regards ventilation, the temperature can be kept under control during the warm months nearly as well as if built in other form, thus insuring the greatest product possible during the months of scarcity. The theory of reversing these conditions, and facing the long span from the sun, has not yet been sufficiently proved to be able to speak definitely of the advantages claimed for it.

In regard to the length of a house. For convenience and equal temperature 150 feet is as long as any house should be built, and I consider 125 feet preferable. For width, 18 feet, but some prefer 20 in order to have a walk through the middle bench. This width makes it necessary to support the roof with two sets of purlins, while one is sufficient in an 18 foot house, if the bars are of suitable strength and the glass not over 16 inches wide. Glass 16x20 is a very desirable size, and if of double strength and the best American make, it is good enough. Since natural gas has been used in its manufacture, its quality has greatly increased.

For posts I would use 6x6 red cedar if it is possible to obtain them; if not, then locust, chestnut or white oak. Mark out your corners, set your long posts one at each end, stretch two lines one near the top and the other at the base. Mark for the holes so the posts will not be farther than four feet from centre to centre. If in ordinary firm soil, dig two and one-half feet deep, and set the posts to the lines. Should the soil be soft or spongy, dig the hole three feet deep, and at the bottom place a flat stone. If this is not at hand, fill the first six inches with concrete. Smooth the surface of this and let it harden before setting the posts. If it is desired to carry the water which comes from the roof to any given point, the house should have a fall of at least six inches to 100 feet. Mark the height of your wall on the corner posts, and stretch a taut line from post to post by which mark each for sawing. This is necessary if there is any fall in the house, as in this case the posts will not cut square on their outside face. As a finish for the top of the posts as well as for the formation of a gutter, the most simple as well as the most durable methods are the following. If the house does not have another joined to it on either side, saw the posts

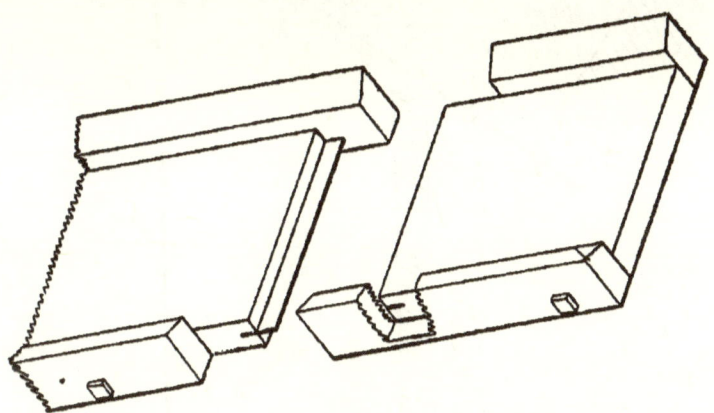

Fig. 2.

to the same bevel as the pitch of your roof. Take two inch plank twelve inches wide, straighten and bring them to a width, square and split the ends with a saw to a depth of one and one-eighth inches. Into this groove drive a piece of band iron two inches by one-eighth, and this will form a tenon, when the plank are driven together in a continuous line. This

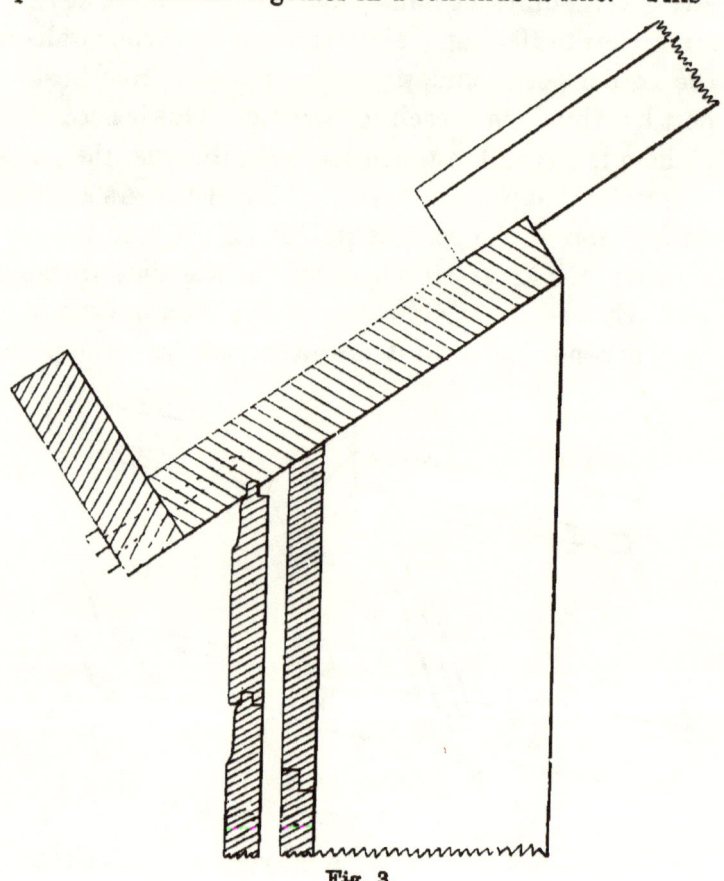

Fig. 3.

will make them water-tight at the joints, if they have been well leaded before putting together, and it does not matter whether the joints come directly over a post or not, as the iron tenons will prevent all warping. See Fig. 2. To form a gutter in this way, where houses do not join each other, take two by six-inch plank, size them, and after having painted the edges to be joined with good thick paint, bolt them on the

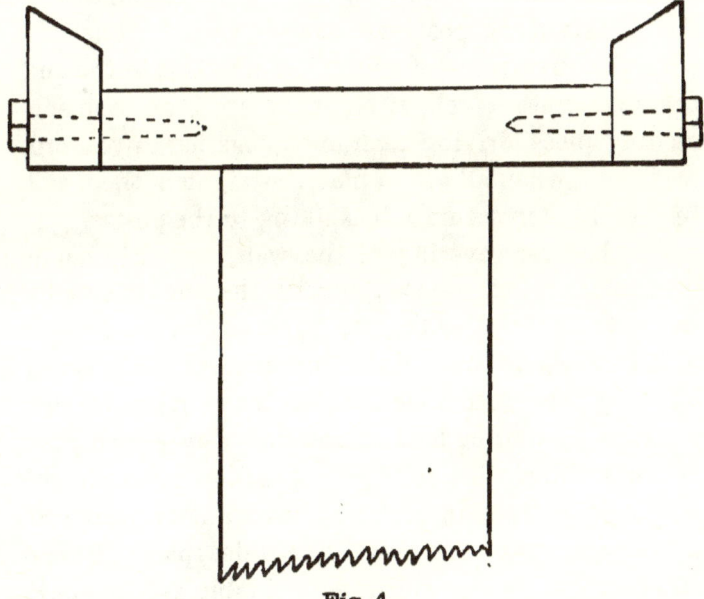

Fig. 4.

lower edge with four-inch lag screws. See Fig. 3. These pieces can be butted together and the joint secured as described in Fig. 2.

The other form where houses join, is to give the top of

the posts a square cut, after which place on them plank as described for the other, on either edge of which bolt two by four pieces that have been dressed on either side and run through a sticker to form the top bevel. See Fig. 4. Throughout the northern states I think as good lumber as can be used in this construction is white pine, and it need not be first clear, as small knots are no detriment, and the sides can be selected from first-class 2x4, being careful that there is no sap on any of them. After the posts are sawed, begin at one end with the first piece of gutter. Spike this to the end post and brace it well, after which bring on each succeeding piece, driving each joint together as you proceed, and when all are in place, straighten them to a line, and fasten securely by spiking to the posts.

For the first covering of the wall, use ship lap or common flooring. Place this with the smooth side in, and with the joint so that no water can find lodgment in it from the interior of the house; cover with heavy building paper (use none that has tar on it) and fasten the same by nailing lath up and down over each post. When finished, this will give a hollow space in the wall half an inch in thickness, which is as good protection against frost as would be a wider space. For an outside covering drop siding is preferable, as it not only makes a good finish, but being tongued and grooved, excludes all air. Use two by eight for the ridge, and when ordering, have a groove three-eighths of an inch deep and of equal width made for the reception of the glass, letting the same be at such a distance from the lower edge, that when the bars are in place, the under surface of both the bars and the ridge will

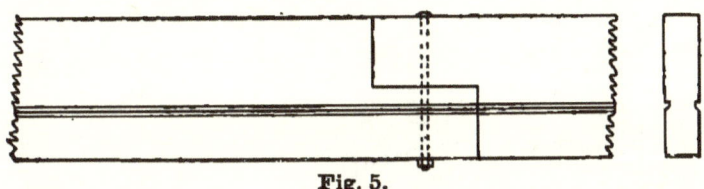

Fig. 5.

be fair. See Fig. 5. This permits the ridge to rise five inches above the bars, which will be found of great advantage when ventilators open at the top.

With the walls complete, it saves labor to construct the benches before putting on the roof, as they can usually be utilized as staging for the superstructure. In the construction of benches there are many kinds of material used. Wood or gas pipe for uprights, slate or tile for the floor. The method adopted will depend mainly upon the amount of money one has to put into their construction. If wood is used for uprights, it is not advisable to use anything but the best cedar, but if this is not at hand, locust, chestnut, white oak or cypress according to their availability.

Fig. 6 shows the usual mode of bench construction in three fourths span houses. This method of building has long been deemed necessary in northern latitudes.

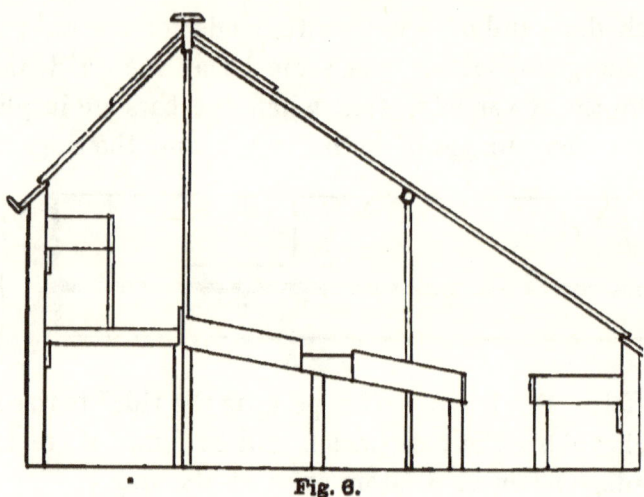

Fig. 6.

A noted grower near New York has recently bu[ilt] a few houses upon a plan differing materially fro[m] that of any others. The frame is iron, built in t[he] usual way—three-fourths span. The north and sou[th] walls, as well as the ends, are also constructed of gla[ss] to within two feet of the ground, and with side ven[ti]lation in both walls. The house is twenty feet [in] width, with two benches, the sides of which are t[wo] feet deep. A path runs all around the house betwe[en] the walls and benches. There is also a path betwe[en] the beds. The main peculiarity consists in the constr[uc]tion of the beds. The first sixteen inches is made [of] broken stone, through the center of which three o[ne] inch steam pipes pass at such distances from each oth[er] as to best equalize the distribution of heat. This foundation is then covered with eight inches of soil in which the roses are planted. The following claim is made for this method. Heat being applied to the broken stone by means of the pipes passing through it, renders it possible to use water freely during November and December, and this overcomes, in a measure, the difficulty experienced in inciting a rapid growth during those months by the usual methods. The writer would only add that in February it was his pleasure to examine these houses, and the growth of foliage would seem to substantiate the claim made.

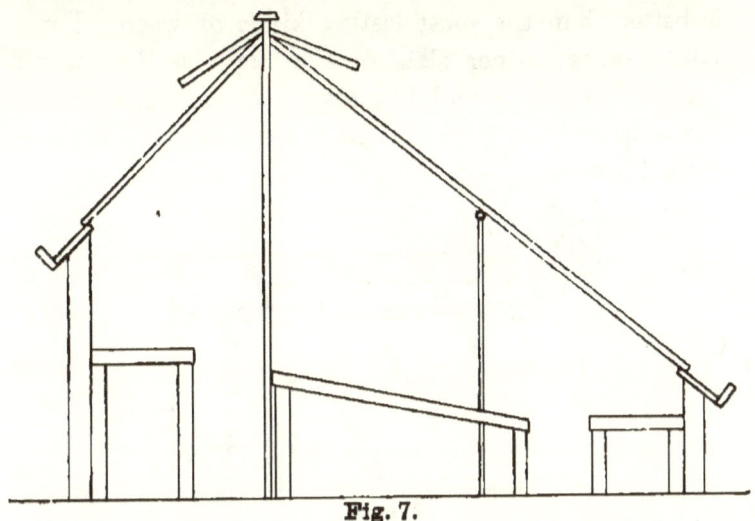

Fig. 7.

Another method of bench construction, as shown in Fig. 7, is preferred by some, as it gives more head room to tall, strong growing varieties.

Gas pipe in bench construction, though expensive at first, is durable. So also is that made of rejected street car rails, and when such can be obtained at the cost of old iron they are not very expensive. Angle iron has also been used by some, but one grower who built with it tells me he thinks its life not long enough to repay the outlay, as it rusts and scales rapidly.

Whatever the method adopted, let no part of the weight of the bench be borne by the walls. This is of great importance. The side benches can be fastened to the walls as a means of bracing, but shores should be provided to carry the benches, otherwise the weight will soon throw the gutter out of a straight line. For the bottoming of benches, nothing in my estimation, is better than the most lasting kinds of wood. For pot growing, either slate or tile may be the most economical in the end, but for cut flowers, tile slabs dry so quickly as to make their use hazardous in unskilled hands.

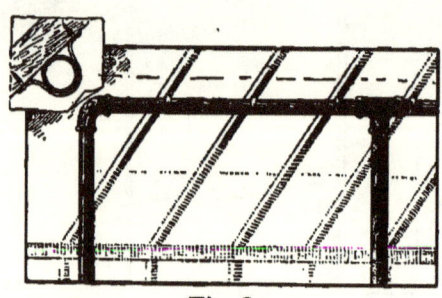

Fig. 8.

GREENHOUSE CONSTRUCTION. 13

For a purlin, inch pipe is neat and strong. See Fig. 8. Let it be supported by uprights every eight feet, and see that they rest on a solid base, a stone or small brick pier. Before glazing, the purlin should be fastened to each bar by means of screws and a narrow band of sheet iron or tin. The ridge should be supported by inch and a quarter pipe. Iron plates are kept in stock

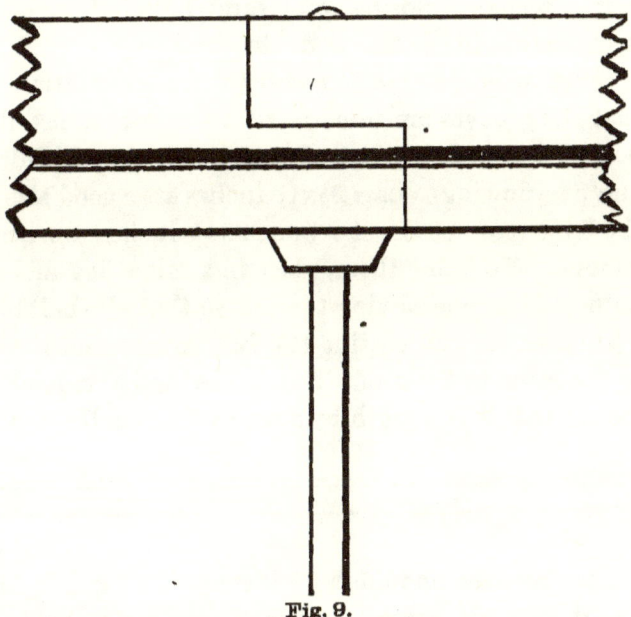

Fig. 9.

by builders which can be fastened to the ridge and the pipe secured to them by a thread. In the absence of these, substitutes may be easily made of hard wood as shown in Fig. 9. A hole of suitable size is bored in

the wood to receive the thread of the pipe, and
wood is then fastened by means of screws to the rid

These iron supports to the ridge should not be o
seven feet apart, and it is well to construct the ridge
14 foot lengths, as in this way one of the supports
be placed directly under each joint. As a large port
of the weight of a roof is carried by these uprights,
foot of each should rest on a solid foundation, oth
wise they will settle, and the building spread.
grooved bars are used to convey the condensation,
that the grooves are smooth before painting, else th
will be a constant source of annoyance, through fill
and overflowing. Bars $2\frac{1}{2} \times 1\frac{3}{8}$ inches are a good size
the long roof, for the short one $2 \times 1\frac{3}{8}$ inches are hea
enough. To frame them, place in a mitre box and
both ends before moving the bar, so that all shall be
a uniform length, cutting the foot square and the
to the bevel of the roof. Notch the under side of
foot $1\frac{3}{4}$ inches in length by a depth that shall leave

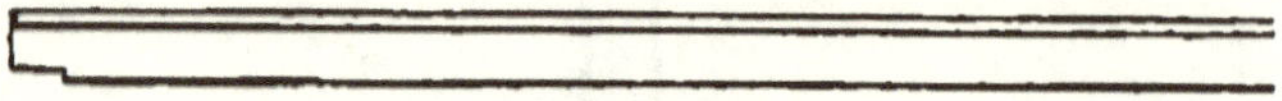

Fig. 10.

timber between shoulders $1\frac{3}{8}$ inches. See Fig. 10. A
all are framed, before joining them, stand the lov
ends in tubs of boiled linseed oil, three inches de
and when dry give the whole roof two coats of the b
white lead and pure linseed oil.

GREENHOUSE CONSTRUCTION. 15

To erect the roof commence at one end of the building, raise one length of the ridge, putting bars on either side at each end, fasten those at the end of the building permanently, the others temporarily, so that should your ridge not be straight, it can be lowered or raised as you proceed to place the bars in position. When using a continuous ventilator let one-third of the bars run to the roof—and these should be put up first—in doing which use a gauge sufficiently long to allow for three rows of glass with their short bars between.

As soon as one section of ridge is complete, plumb it by drawing a line from plate to plate at the base of the first set of bars, dropping a plumb line from the top of the same bar and vary until the lines touch. Brace securely and proceed to erect in the same manner the rest of the roof. After setting the long bars have some head-

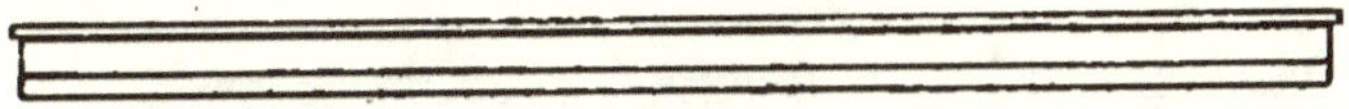

Fig. 11.

ers prepared (Fig. 11), of suitable length and thickness to fill in between them, for the support of the shorter bars on the same side, and if the upper surface of this header is as wide as can be made from two inch stock it will serve to hinge the ventilators on if they are to open at the top. With a short gauge (See Fig. 12), set your shorter bars. Fill in between these, where

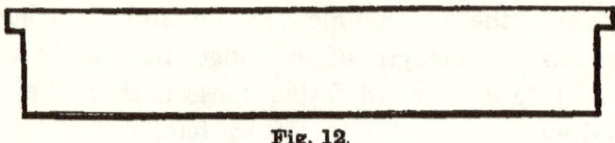

Fig. 12.

they rest on the plate, with pieces prepared for the purpose, cutting them to their place one by one, for as there will be a slight variation in the distance between the bars these pieces cannot all be cut to a length beforehand. See Fig. 13. Dip the freshly cut ends in paint

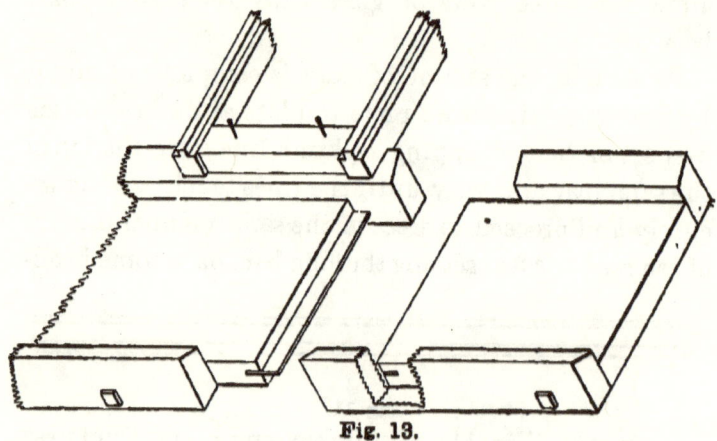

Fig. 13.

and fasten in place. Then run a gauge from the inner surface of these that will mark one-fourth of an inch from the edge and two inches from each bar, drive heavy one inch wire nails for the end of the first glass to rest against, and after the purlin is in place and fastened, you are ready to glaze.

Double thick glass, 16x20, is too heavy to lap in the usual way and keep in place. Neither is butted glass desirable on account of the great amount of leakage, but this can be obviated by using a zinc joint, an invention of Mr. J. M. Gasser, of Cleveland, Ohio. See Fig. 14. I have used these for several seasons, as I have been repairing, and like them very much.

Fig. 14.

Where the glass is not lapped, as is the case when these joints are used, the putty can be applied to the bars with a machine, saving the work of two men, and again, after the glass is set, the corners can be drawn on the outside by the same process, filling any space there may be at the edge of the glass, thus making a perfectly tight roof. As fast as the glass is laid it should be fastened with glazier's points, No. 00, as its weight will otherwise cause it to buckle and slide.

I once heard a careless workman say, "paint and putty are great rectifiers," and while open joints are to be deprecated, should they occur through accident or otherwise, see that they are carefully filled, and that all nails about the gutters are well set and the holes puttied before giving the final coat of paint. Every season as the houses are replanted, the gutters, both inside and out, as well as the foot of the bars where they join the gutter, should be given a coat of paint. All the roof work should be given a thorough cleaning and painting once in two years, and some consider it economy to paint thoroughly every year, because every particle of light that can be obtained during the winter months is desirable, and both cleaning and painting add so largely to this result, that one or both should be adopted.

CHAPTER II.

VENTILATION, HOW CONSTRUCTED.

First, I would have it continuous on the south roof, and from 20 to 36 inches wide. Never ventilate on the north side unless hinged at the top, otherwise, when open, the sun will be admitted in such a way as to burn the plants on the north bench. An error of this kind will necessitate the protection of the bench by shading with some thin material like cheese cloth under the ventilator, and as far as the opening extends, as the writer has found from experience. These continuous ventilators can be made of various lengths, according to the size of glass used. It is usual to hinge them at the bottom, and if the upper edges are doweled, all will move alike when raised, and the opening will be uniform throughout the entire length of the house. For raising and lowering this there is but one way, and that by some of the various machines constructed for the purpose.

In addition to this, I would have at least eight ventilators on the north side of a house 125 feet long, if continuous ventilation is not used on this side. These can be made in the form of sash, and of varying sizes, according to the size of glass used. Hinge these at the ridge and they will be found exceedingly convenient in airing when the wind is blowing from the south, also for maintaining a low summer temperature. As these ventilators will rest on the top of the bars, they can be made wind-tight by fastening a continuous piece of quarter round on their under surface, in such a manner that when shut, the round will be inside the opening, thus covering any crack or opening made by the warping or springing of the ventilator. It not being necessary to use these small ventilators as often as the main ones, it is optional with the builder as to the best way of raising or lowering them. If it is not deemed desirable to run two lines of shafting, they can be opened and closed in the old way, by means of an iron lift, in which holes have been made at varying distances. But whatever the method, I would not be without them, as they are needed from July to November. Still another and a better way—if it can be afforded—is to have continuous ventilators on each side, making each ventilator of a suitable width to receive one light twenty inches long. Hang these at the ridge for rose houses, and you will always have a system that will be the best possible preventive of mildew, so far as ventilating is concerned, while both openings can be used to advantage through the heated term. This of course necessitates two lines of shafting and a double apparatus for lifting the two lines of ventilators. For carnations I would advise continuous ventilators three feet in width, the south one to open at the ridge, the north one to be hung to the ridge. These, with wall ventilation on either side will give a fine circulation of air.

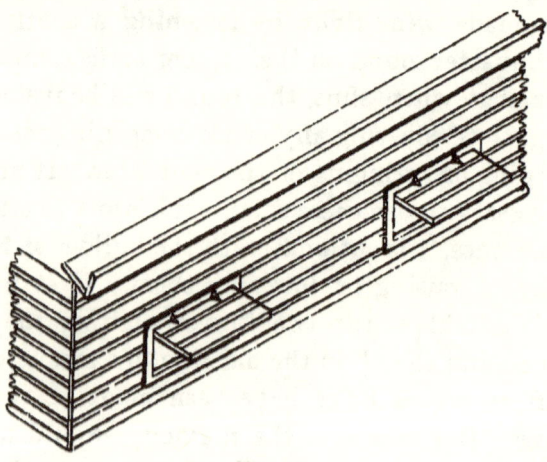

Fig. 15.

For summer work in houses adapted to the growth of cut flowers, I consider wall ventilation indispensable, and for this reason would never join houses used for this purpose, but place them far enough apart so that the ridge of one will not shade the south bench of the one north of it during the short days of winter. On level ground they should be from 15 to 18 feet apart, according to their height, but if on a slope the distance can be lessened in proportion to its declivity. Each house should be connected at one end with a work room, and if several houses are built it is very convenient to have this room in the centre, but its roof should be low in order that it may produce the least amount of shade. While building the walls, if such ventilation cannot be provided as in Fig. 16, put in at least every 12 feet, a frame 12 inches wide in the clear, and of a length that will fill the space between two posts. See Fig. 15. This frame should be of sufficient depth to admit of a temporary filling on the inside for winter use, while the door for the outside may be constructed of the same material as the rest of the wall, and hinged so that when shut it shall be fair with its face. These side ventilators should be placed in both the north and south walls, and directly against the line of pipes, but under rather than over them. In this way, they can be used at times of the year when the air as it enters the house will be tempered by passing over the pipes. This is of course on the supposition that the pipes are filled with water that has not had time to cool.

One grower has recently built a house, in the north wall of which he has placed at intervals of 20 feet, regular doors. These are 6x2½ feet, and instead of being placed up and down in the wall are horizontal, and as high as can be opened and swing under the eaves. These are for the double purpose of ventilation, and for convenience in emptying and filling the benches.

Where houses are needed exclusively for the summer growing of cut flowers a roof of equal span and from 11 to 12 feet in width is preferable. These can be built in the same way as already described, only that I would make all the rafters the full length of the roof, and have the ventilation continuous on both sides, hanging each line at the ridge. I do not like a western exposure for any house, and think the sun takes stronger effect on such a house from 1 to 5 P. M. in summer, than it does from 10 to 2 o'clock on a southern face. The best varieties to plant for the purpose of summer flowering and their treatment will be described hereafter.

CHAPTER III.

THE SHORT SPAN TO THE SOUTH.

Fig. 16 gives a good idea of the latest style of building. This is from a photograph of two houses built last fall by the well known carnation grower, Mr. Fred Dorner, of La Fayette, Ind. If lack of ground space renders it necessary to build continuously, this plan will give less shade than when reversed, but if necessary to build together, it would be far better not to join more than two houses as seen in the illustration. This will admit of wall ventilation on each side of the two.

This innovation upon existing and tried methods has been viewed with great incredulity by the profession at large, and I must confess that I have also been skeptical as to its practicability. It is unquestioned, however, that mere prejudice should not deter us from surrounding ourselves with whatever will contribute to the highest success, and this has led me to investigate the new system by visiting some who have adopted it. I am told on good authority—though I have not visited the place—that the gentleman with whom the idea originated, and who had such phenomenal success the first season, has since changed growers, and that this success passed out of the same door and at the same time, as did the man under whose watchful eye it was obtained. However this may be, there are some features in this mode of construction which commend themselves while

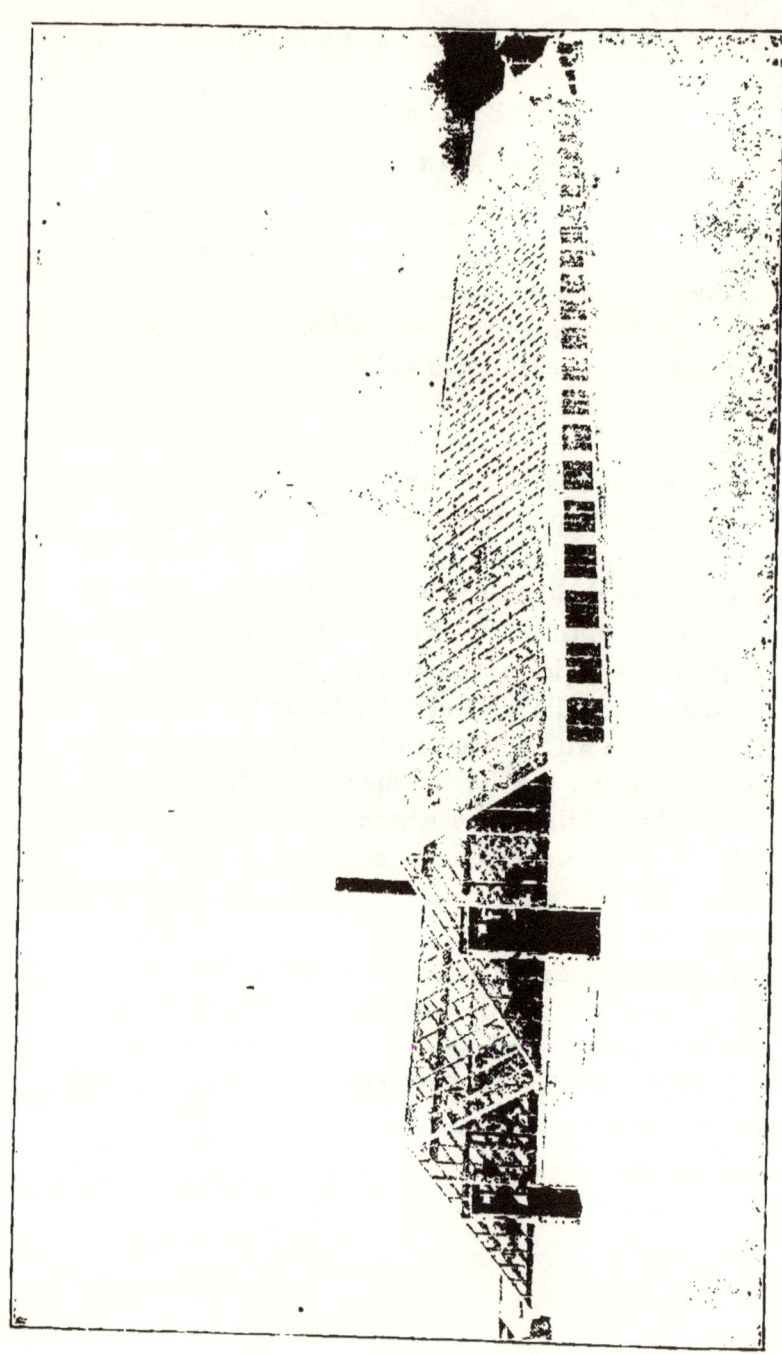

Fig. 16.

there are others which awaken distrust; nor will the objection produced by these features be removed from the mind without further investigation and trial.

The claim for this method of building is, that the short span and the sun are at right angles during the shortest days, and that this position admits the greatest amount of sunlight and warmth, while the more either the sun or glass vary from a right angle, just in that proportion are the sun's rays deflected and the heat lessened. The feeling of the sun upon the face and person as it comes through the sharp roof, is both marked and pleasant, as compared with that of a roof at the common angle, and so far as appearances go, would seem to prove the theory correct. The roof being so steep, snow cannot remain upon it, and it is quickly free from frost on a sunny day, though the air is keen outside. Added to this is the fact that owing to the sharpness of the roof the strain on the bars lessens as they approach the perpendicular, rendering it possible to use less wood and more glass, thus securing the maximum amount of light.

On the other hand, if the weather is severe the north roof is a sheet of snow and frost, and this is removed only as the heat from the interior melts it, no rays of the sun touching its exterior surface during the entire day. This state of things of course causes the plants to turn toward the light, but how much it has a tendency to draw them in long continued cold weather, the writer is unable to say.

My visit to Mr. Dorner was during the severe weather of January, and at that time I suggested to him a trial of temperature between this and a three-fourths span house, on some day when artificial heat could be dispensed with. Under date of January 30th he gives me the following result: "On the basis of the temperature being the same in both houses fifteen minutes after steam was shut off, the house having the short span to the south at the end of an hour had gained six degrees on the other, the test being made by keeping the thermometer in the shade."

Fig. 17.

At another place visited by the writer where this method is being used, a portion of the benefit sought was lost through faulty construction, the gutters being so high as to cast a shade of six feet at 3 P. M. This together with the result of observations elsewhere, leads me to the conclusion that were I to build a house for myself as an experiment, it would be as shown by an end view in Fig. 17. Nothing should join it on either side, and if for carnations, it should have wall ventilation on each side, and continuous on both the north and south roof, the south ventilator being hinged at the bottom, the north at the top. For roses, the same in every respect save that both continuous ventilators would be hinged at the ridge.

Mr. Dorner feels that he obtains more light during the short days under the new system than with the old, and about the only criticism I could find when there, aside from the frost on the long roof, was that the south gutter cast a shade during the latter part of the day on benches built low enough to be handy. This could be obviated by lowering the south gutter as far as it can be and leave room for a foot of ventilation between it and the ground.

With all the facts it has been possible to obtain up to the present time, for my own use I would not feel justified in changing the old style for the new until the latter has been more thoroughly tested.

Still another plan is advocated by some, which does away with the objection found in the system last mentioned, so far, as snow and frost are concerned. I know of but one grower who has adopted this style of building, but there may be others. This gentleman thinks he finds in it the advantages claimed for the former method, with none of its disadvantages. Fig. 18 gives an end view of this house. Dimensions, 16 feet inside measurement between posts. Height to under side of ridge, 14 feet. Walls 2 feet 6 inches.

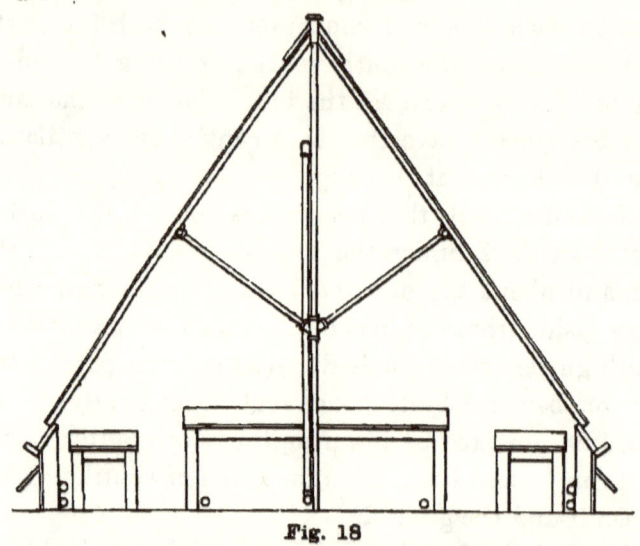

Fig. 18

If the side benches are used for planting, they should be built as near the ground as possible and have a space of two or three inches between the ground and the bottom of the bench. Two pipes are hung on each wall, and the radiation from them is prevented from reaching the plants by ceiling the back of each side bench about 18 inches. This will also prevent air from the side ventilators from coming in direct contact with the plants. If large glass is used, each roof should be supported by purlins of one-inch gas pipe, and braces of the same material can be made to support them by connecting them with the iron supports of the roof, which should be of two-inch pipe. Seven pipes for heating are used in this house, one of which is in the roof, three feet below the ridge through which the flow is carried, returning in six pipes of the same size, as seen in Fig. 18. Instead of facing directly south, if built to face s. s. east, it is claimed that both the morning and afternoon sun will have the greatest effect, or rather, will be more equally divided.

I should hesitate to build in this way, unless the two side benches could be used for small pot plants. In this case, if these were built two feet wide and near the glass, it would permit of an eight foot bench in the middle of the house which would no doubt do splendid work.

CHAPTER IV.

GREENHOUSE HEATING.

The problem connected with this much agitated question, has been solved to the entire satisfaction of the advocates of the different systems time and time again, and still, one who would commence anew is as much in the dark as ever, as to which is the best for him to adopt. Climate, fuel and space enter largely into the decision of the question in each individual case. There is no question but that the ideal method is by steam generated by natural gas, both for its cleanliness as well as the ease with which it is cared for when once in working order. To only a few highly favored individuals has this great boon been given, while the rest of us must see much of the profits roll into the furnace in the form of "trust" anthracite, or if we seek a cheaper article and fall back upon bituminous coal, we are not only sufferers ourselves, but our neighbors, if we have any, proclaim us a nuisance. But notwithstanding dust, dirt, and ribald tongue, we must each burn what is the most economical, for the profits are not large, as many suppose them to be, and our product must enter the markets in competition with that of men of wealth to whom it matters little whether their investment pays expenses or not, so long as they personally have what they wish to use, and can sell enough to help out on the salary of the gardener.

The question of fuel must largely control the kind of boiler we adopt. If natural gas, then a marine will be found to be a great heat producer. If anthracite, such as have proved to be the most economical in the sections where that coal is used. If bituminous, such boilers must be selected as will produce the best combustion and thus aid the fireman in his efforts to keep the smoke at a minimum.

The original method of heating, now nearly obsolete, was by means of brick flues, and while the more common plants can be grown in this manner, for fine work this method is useless, and unworthy the space necessary to describe it.

CHAPTER V.

HOT WATER HEATING.

Hot water is used in three forms. The first and original method of laying pipes, consisted in having the flow rise gradually from the boiler to the extreme end of the house, a rise of one foot in one hundred being deemed sufficient. At this point an expansion or standpipe was usually placed, and from it the water returned to the boiler in another set of pipes, having the same fall as the flow had elevation.

The pipe used in this system is four-inch cast iron in lengths of about five feet, and a quick and durable way to put this together is as follows:

Buy a coil of eight strand, inch and a quarter hemp rope. Cut this in lengths that will allow a strand to go twice around the pipe. Put this once around the joint and tamp it lightly. Between this and the next layer of hemp, put about the same quantity of Portland cement as you have of rope. The cement should be of the consistency of good putty. Tamp in another strand of hemp. This, when well tamped, will fill the joint within about half an inch of the top. After putting together several joints in this way, finish with cement in the same way as you would if you were using red lead, and you will have a much cheaper joint, and one that will be as durable as any, providing care is taken to use nothing but the best Portland cement

It will be obvious to any builder, that the rests should be in position and the pipe all laid before the benches are erected. The number of pipes necessary will depend of course on the location. Seven is none too many and eight for all localities north of the fortieth parallel

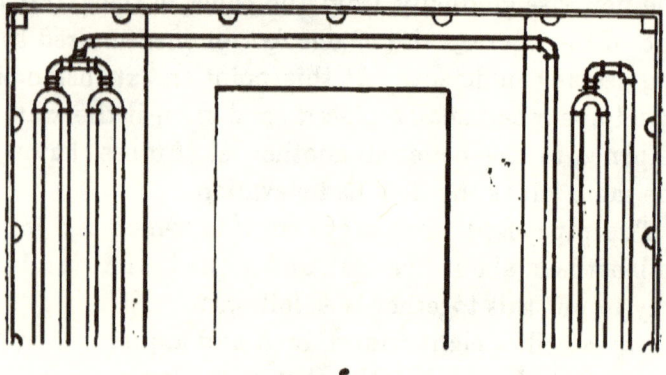

Fig. 19.

the house being eighteen or twenty feet in width. The first cost is a little more, but it insures fully against great falls in temperature to which all sections are liable, and while five pipes will do the work in ordinary weather, there are a few days in nearly every season when they will all be needed, and the saving effected by not having the plants given a check, will oftentimes in one season compensate for the extra expense.

To lay these pipes, carry one flow nearly to the extreme end of your north bench (See Fig. 19), and return it in two pipes laid directly south of it. Put a valve on this flow at some convenient point near where it enters the house, and these three pipes can be used at will. Carry another flow under the south side of the same bench to within one foot of the extreme end, put on an ell and carry across the end of the house, bring the water back under the south bench in four pipes, and when these approach the boiler they may be united in one and returned to it in that form.

In this way you have your heat on the outside of your house for the entire distance, leaving the space under the middle bench clear and free. I have noticed that if the circulation is carried up and down a house without crossing the end farthest from the boiler, several feet of that end will be cooler than any other part of the house, causing dampness to be driven there, and a consequent condensation of moisture on the foliage during the night, which will soon cause the leaves to fall.

The inlets to a boiler should always be greater than the outlet, and it is customary to use them in the proportion of a four-inch outlet or flow to two inlets or returns of the same size. If the boiler is of suitable capacity to carry several houses, it will facilitate the cir[culation] lation to have the outlet six inches, and carried b[y a] pipe of the same size as a header, from which all [the] four-inch flows may be taken.

Should it seem advisable to adopt this, as it is term[ed] "the up hill system," it will be necessary to obse[rve] four things:

First. That your boiler is set low enough, so that [the] point from which the water flows out of it shall be [at] least twelve inches lower than where the flow p[ipe] commences to return to the boiler.

Second. That at the highest point of the flow th[ere] be a vent for the escape of air. This may be provi[ded] for by a regulation stand pipe. A simple way is [to] tap the casting at that point and screw into it a [half] inch gas pipe, letting its end be a few inches hig[her] than your expansion tank, or by a simple pet c[ock] which can be opened and closed at will.

Third. That neither the flow nor return be allo[wed] to make short dips or depressions from the settlin[g of] the rests, as by this means the circulation is someti[mes] impeded, but that the pipes be so graded that the [rise] and fall will be as nearly uniform as possible.

Fourth. That what is called an "expansion tan[k"] be placed at some convenient point near the boi[ler.] This may vary in size from one-fourth to a full bar[rel] according to the amount of pipe it is expected to se[rve,] a barrel being as large as will be needed for any o[f] nary sized boiler. Connect this barrel by means of an inch pipe with your return just before it enters the boiler, and all waste of water in the circulation can be supplied from this point. Should the flow at its highest point not be supplied with a stand pipe, it is best to tap the flow as it leaves the boiler, inserting an inch pipe and carrying it over and just into the top of the expansion tank. This will not only allow air to escape, but should the fires be crowded so that steam is generated, it can escape at this point and what is termed "kicking" pipes will be avoided. As to the height of this tank, the bottom of it should always be higher than the highest part of any of the pipes.

CHAPTER VI.

THE DOWN HILL SYSTEM.

The second system of hot water heating is what is called the "down hill system," and differs from the one just described in that the water is raised to the highest point at once, and from that point gradually falls until it reaches the boiler again. This gives an opportunity for overhead heating, which for some crops is beneficial, while to others it is detrimental.

To lay these pipes, commence with the flow, raising it perpendicularly from the boiler, to such a height as will permit you to carry the main from which your flows are taken, over your doorways. From your highest upright point, let the pipes fall gradually all the way round. If you use a barrel for expansion, let the bottom of it be a little above the top of the flow. Connect it with the return as described already, tapping

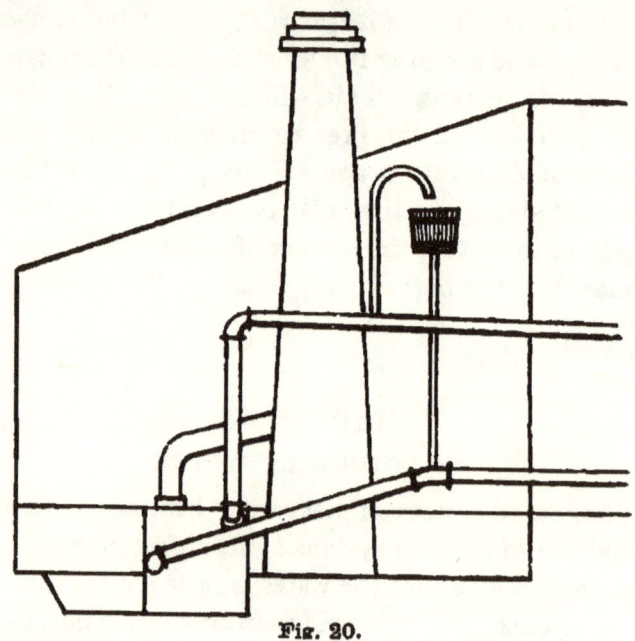

Fig. 20.

the highest point on the flow pipe and carrying thence an inch pipe over and into the top of the barrel. See Fig. 20.

It is also well to have one or more pet cocks at other points, in order to facilitate the exit of air when filling the pipes.

Two things can be said in favor of this system. It permits of setting the boiler on the surface of the ground. It can be used in the growth of such crops as are benefited by overhead heat.

CHAPTER VII.
HOT WATER UNDER PRESSURE.

The third system is that of hot water under pressure, and requires that both pipe and boiler be of wrought iron, if the pressure is over twenty pounds.

Two inch gas pipes are commonly used for this and they may be laid as already described, on the "down hill" plan; but for this no expansion tank is required.

This system is practicable only when it can be connected with water pressure, either public or private, and should not be less than ten pounds as indicated by a steam gauge.

If you have city water works, carry an inch pipe from the coldest part of your boiler—which is usually the rear and near the bottom—connecting the same at some convenient point with the hydrant. This will constitute your expansion tank, and the amount of pressure you can carry on your boiler without emptying it, will be a fraction *less* than a gauge will indicate as being the pressure of the hydrant water.

If a higher degree of pressure is maintained on the

boiler than the water works give, the result will be empty your boiler and pipes into the hydrant. Wh[en] a valve is essential on the pipe connecting the hydra[nt] with the boiler, *it must always be left open* when the boi[ler] is in use. Do not commit the error of a brother flor[ist] who was also searching for "purchased wit," and [be]cause the fire was moving the water towards and i[n] the hydrant, shut the valve!—the result of his expe[ri]ment being, that the next time he looked at his boi[ler] the pressure was above danger point, and had not ve[nt] been given at once and the fire raked out, boiler, hou[se] and all would have traveled skywards.

To insure a free circulation, connect a stand pi[pe] with the flow at its highest point near the boil[er]. This should be of the same size as the pipe with whi[ch] it is connected, and from three to five feet long. Cl[ose] the top securely, tap and screw into its highest po[int] an automatic air cock, in order that all air may be [ex]pelled as fast as it gathers.

Marvelous figures were given, a few years since, [of] the saving in pipe by this method over the other t[wo], but experience does not substantiate them. I ha[ve] found seven two-inch pipes none too many to mainta[in] a temperature of 65 degrees in a house twelve feet wi[de] and for one eighteen feet wide, sixteen are used. T[his] is more than twice the amount of pipe needed wh[en] the circulating medium is steam.

CHAPTER VIII.
HEATING BY STEAM.

The fourth and last system is that of steam. To give all the various methods advocated for steam heating would of itself require a larger volume than this. For this reason only a few general principles can be given, leaving the builder to apply them to any particular system he may choose to adopt.

First, the boiler should have a power of at least 50 per cent. in excess of what will be demanded of it in all ordinary weather, and more is better. What is true of this, is true of all heat generators. Time and coal are largely economized by having a capacity for heat far in excess of the need. For instance, if you are satisfied a boiler costing $300 will do your work with close attention, add $200 more to it and let your fire burn naturally, thus reducing much coal to ashes that otherwise would go out of the stoke hole in the form of coke and charred coal. These rules apply in the main to boilers in which a cheap grade of bituminous coal is used. Having had less experience in burning anthracite I cannot speak intelligently of its requirements.

It is not uncommon for a boiler, especially if old or second hand, to fail at a time when needed most, and it is mistaken economy to ever set any but those newly made, and in which the best of material has been used. Even in this case, some prefer to insure themselves against loss by setting two, each of them being of sufficient capacity to do the work required, but so connected that a change can be made at short notice in case a flue should collapse, or for any other reason one should become disabled. Many years ago, an accident of this kind occurred with the writer, and had it not been that it was during a "January thaw" when the thermometer did not fall below 60 at any time during the six days required for repairs, it would have been a serious matter and resulted in great loss. At the time alluded to, the work was being done by one thirty horse power locomotive boiler. One morning a crack was found in the crown sheet, from which water enough soon escaped to render firing impossible. Examination developed the fact that between the bars which held it in position, a deposit of scale and mud had formed, sufficient to prevent water from reaching the sheet and counteracting the heat of the fire. This fact is cited to show that whatever our heating system, boilers should be carefully examined every season before commencing a winter's work.

The second thing to be observed is the setting of your boiler. A perfect circulation of steam should be obtained with a pressure of two pounds or less, and it is desirable to return the condensation directly to the boiler without the intervention of traps or pumps of any kind. To do this, it is necessary to have the boiler lower than the return pipes. If you are building on descending ground, have your boiler pit at the lowest point. If on level ground, let your pit be deep enough so the top of the boiler will be two or three feet lower than are your returns at any point where they leave your houses and are connected with a main ready to be dropped perpendicularly or otherwise, and be connected with the boiler at its lowest point. This will give a fall of from six to ten feet according to the size and kind of boiler you use, and is essential to a perfect circulation.

Third, see that your main pipe from which all the lesser mains are fed, is of sufficient size. A boiler of sufficient capacity to feed 10,000 feet of $1\frac{1}{4}$ inch pipe should have a six-inch distributing main 15 feet long, when it may be reduced to 4 inches, and this should extend as far as the combined width of your houses, whether you feed them all from one end, or whether the distribution is made each way from a central house. The size of the connecting mains will depend upon the length and size of the house. Two inches is sufficient to feed six two-inch returns, or nine one and one-quarter inch. If radiation is not wanted from this pipe it, as well as the six-inch, should be well protected by some of the best forms of covering. The main which feeds the house should be carried to its extreme end and from that point distributed into as many returns as are necessary to keep the temperature at the degree desired. For a house eighteen feet wide one two-inch flow and six two-inch returns, or one two-inch flow and nine one and one-quarter inch returns will maintain a temperature of 60° when the outside temperature is twenty below zero.

From the point where the main feed leaves the four or six inch pipe, all the pipes should have a fall until connected again with the boiler, and the point where they emerge from the house on their return should be supplied with air cocks. These should all be closed as soon as circulation is fully established. As the returns emerge from the houses connect them with a three-inch pipe, but place this last named pipe below the water line of the boiler before the returns are connected with it. It can then be joined to the base of the boiler. Although not absolutely necessary, it is probably better to carry the main feed of a house down the centre, and from twelve to fifteen inches below the ridge. As before mentioned, if radiation from this pipe is not desired, it can very easily be retained by asbestos or other covering. A careful observance of all these points is necessary to a perfect circulation. The valves and checks necessary to the control of the circulating medium are well known to all steam fitters and need not be enumerated here.

I am sometimes asked the question which of all these systems I like the best, and which I would advise a beginner to adopt. This last question cannot be answered definitely, for reasons already stated, and as to the first, I can only give my own experience.

Heating by Steam.

For ten years and more prior to the general introduction of steam for greenhouse heating I was conversant with its use, but in a more imperfect form in some respects than as used at the present time. In the growth of cut flowers for the past ten years, hot water in its various forms has been used by me exclusively. I am unable to say, however, by actual test, which of the two systems will produce the best results, as I have had no opportunity to try them in comparison and under equal circumstances.

The consensus of opinion undoubtedly favors the use of steam on large places, and while it may be best to equip a new and large range of houses in this way, I have not as yet seen it to be to my interest to change a system that works satisfactorily, as that change must necessarily mean a large sacrifice of material in the process of reconstruction.

On the other hand, if your place is small, you will doubtless find the old system of hot water to require less care and trouble in the production of good results.

CHAPTER IX.

OVERHEAD HEATING.

For growing roses, I am satisfied that "overhead heating" is a positive injury, unless the pipes are at such a distance from the plants that the radiation will not foster spider. The distance not being less than that of the main feed pipe near the ridge previously described. But that it is beneficial to some crops has been demonstrated in my own experience. In the growth of carnations, I consider a portion of the heat thus applied of positive benefit, as it helps to dry the foliage at a season of the year when artificial means are necessary. For the growth of small roses in pots, this method is also of great value, and were I piping my houses anew, I should provide an extra pipe over every bench used for this purpose, arranging it so as to be under perfect control, to be used or not, as seemed necessary.

A knowledge of the benefit derived from this method came to me by accident. In the winter of '91, being crowded for room, I removed the contents of a north bench which had been occupied by "Wabans" (more experience) and filled it with young pot plants that had been potted about three weeks, and which up to date had been given what is considered the best room in a house, a south bench near the glass. The bench to which they were removed was fully three feet from the glass, and partially shaded by a rank growth of roses on a middle bench south of it. Directly under the gutter was a four-inch hot water main running the entire length of the house, and notwithstanding it was in January when sun heat is scarce, the radiation from this main evaporated all dampness and moisture from the plants, rendering it possible to syringe often, and to produce under these seemingly unfavorable circumstances, a health and vigor of growth seldom seen at that season of the year, even under the best possible conditions.

CHAPTER X.

ROSES.

THEIR CULTIVATION, DISEASES, ETC.

No other plant is to-day so largely grown for cut flowers as the rose. Nor is there another upon which so much time and thought has been expended in its development, or in its perfection. The short season during which roses are sold at a profit renders it imperative that he who would make the most of that period, must avail himself of every facility which will contribute to success. To this end essays have from time to time been called for from the most successful growers. Discussions calculated to bring to the surface thoughts born of experience have been called out, and while in this way many valuable facts and suggestions have been brought to our attention, still each grower has had to act largely upon his own judgment, and draw conclusions in the main from his own experience.

I well remember the eager anticipation with which I listened to the first essay on this subject, as well as the unsatisfied hunger and disappointment with which I turned away at its close, simply because I did not find in it the solution of the one question above all others which was then troubling me. In the light of subsequent events I can see that it was all clear to the mind of the essayist, and that he could not have known the conditions which constituted a failure with me, while with him, seemingly, similar conditions were a success.

As this line of thought tends directly to the use of soils, and as my belief increases with each passing year, that on them, and on their adaptability to the needs of the different varieties of roses we grow, depends, in no small degree, our success, it seems to me wise to commence with what may be truly considered the foundation stones of our superstructure.

CHAPTER XI.
SOIL.

The impression at one time prevailed to a considerable extent that a chemical analysis would reveal what was lacking to make a perfect soil, and that this ingredient could be supplied artificially. Unfortunately, experiments in this line only went to prove that Dame Nature resented any such interference with her secret laboratory, so that observation and experiment seem to be the only means at our command with which to prove their adaptability for producing certain desired results.

For ten years past, no one rose has been cultivated so extensively, as Perle des Jardins, and still in some localities it cannot be grown with any degree of success. In fact it has been discarded by some prominent growers for that reason.

Where I am located, the soil is a rich loam with a slight mixture of sand, and has a sandy clay subsoil, but not of sufficient strength for the manufacture of either brick or pottery ware. It is a soil perfectly adapted to the growth of Perle, and in which a crop has never failed to give the best results.

When Catherine Mermet and American Beauty appeared and were given a trial, disappointment was the only result. Both made a magnificent growth, but the Beauties rarely formed a bud, while those that matured on Mermet were so inferior in size and color as to be practically worthless. It was at this stage that I found myself so hungry for the essay already alluded to.

Visits to eastern growers made about this time, revealed the fact that some of them were unable to grow Perle, while other varieties which failed with me, grew there to perfection.

A careful examination and comparison of soils showed theirs to be much firmer and heavier than mine, with a stiff subsoil, through which there was no apparent mixture of sand. This convinced me that herein lay the secret of my failure and their success, but how to supply the needed soil was a knotty problem.

One summer day a short time previous to this, while visiting a brother florist, my attention was called to a magnificent growth of roses, as well as to the peculiar character of the soil in which they were planted. Inquiry elicited the fact, that being out of sod soil, the thought had occurred to him to try a gravelly paste which was found ten feet below the surface. He had discovered this in a bank he was excavating close by in order to make room for another house. No fertilizing material was added, and still the luxuriance of foliage was astonishing. So impressed was I with these results that I took a sample of the soil home with me, and called the attention of my foreman to its peculiar character. Not long after, he brought me one day a soil of similar texture found on our own premises, and upon land hitherto considered worthless. This vein is from one to two feet thick and about six feet below the surface, and consists of both coarse and fine gravel, thoroughly mixed and held together by a sticky, paste-like substance. A trial of this proved it to be the one thing lacking in my soil for the successful growing of certain varieties. Now, with one-third of this added to our natural soil, as good Brides, or Mermets can be grown as are to be found anywhere, while Beauties, instead of climbing out through an aperture in the roof as of old, form buds on a majority of the shoots, which develop into first-class flowers. In order to prove the theory upon which I started, a part of a bench was planted to Perles in which this mixture was used. The growth was grand. Foliage dark and glossy, rich beyond anything I had ever seen, but not one perfect flower was cut from that bench during the entire season, all being what are termed "bullheads." These were grown in a house with Mermets and at the same temperature.

In addition to those varieties mentioned, Madam Hoste, Gontier, and Souv de Wootton, thrive well in this kind of soil, but for La France, Duchess of Albany and Niphetos this mixture is useless, in fact a positive injury.

I have been thus explicit in giving my experience in this matter, because no one can afford to overlook the minutest details while studying soils, and cause and effect connected with their use. Also, because others may find conditions to exist which call for a systematic search not only for the cause, but the remedy.

Those conversant with the black prairie soil of Illinois will have noticed its peculiar texture when wet, and it would seem that it must possess these necessary ingredients. Certain it is, the writer has seen American Beauty in perfect form with some growers who are using this upland sod, and it would seem that if others fail of good results with the same soil, there must be other conditions necessary to success that have not been complied with. These will be considered under their various heads as we proceed.

CHAPTER XII.
STOCK FOR PLANTING.

An important preliminary to planting, is the selection and propagation of the stock we are to use for that purpose. While a general description of the art of propagation and growth of plants is foreign to my purpose, so far as it relates to the subject matter under consideration, I think it of sufficient importance to claim our earnest thought. With good stock, planted at the proper time, succeeding steps are comparatively easy. With medium or inferior plants at the start, it is an uphill fight all the way through, and a consequent loss.

The class of wood to be used for cuttings, is in my estimation, an important matter. I am aware that this has given rise to much controversy of late, but notwithstanding the opinions given by some of our best growers, I still claim that an indiscriminate use of wood in propagating—if we would obtain the best results—is a mistake. When practicable to do so, I would never use anything but clean healthy shoots terminated by buds. Reject absolutely, all "trimmings" or weak growth, and have as little to do with blind wood as possible. It stands to reason, that a succession of the best will gradually raise the standard of excellence. We know this to be true in animal life. It has also been proved in various ways in the vegetable kingdom. All know the unswerving law of heredity in the human organism. The sooner we apply these proved principles to matters horticultural the more rapid will be our approach to the ideal standard.

The propagation of roses from blind wood may show no appreciable evil results for one, two or three years. But let him who would demonstrate it thoroughly persist in the use of this wood alone for ten or fifteen years, and we shall then know whether the tendency is to depreciate the blooming qualities of the stock or not. As for myself, I have no desire to experiment in that direction, preferring to use such as I know will bring satisfactory results.

No practical man will attempt to improve any species

either in the animal or vegetable kingdom, by reproducing them through the medium of inferior parentage. But a prominent grower once said to me, "You are unfair in your premises; plants are not governed by any such laws." Let us look into the matter.

Some time since, while examining the plants in the Botanical Garden at Washington, my attention was called to one, with the request that I name it. It resembled a familiar variety, but was so far superior in every way that I hesitated to call it by name. It proved to be what it seemed, Ficus Repens, but so greatly changed by careful selection and the propagation each year for fifteen years, from each year's improvement, as to be scarcely recognized at the end of that time.

If this proved true in this instance and with this plant, why does it not apply to other plants as well? I have felt confident for years that it was one of the factors of success, and am confirmed in this belief through the recently published statement of one of our most intelligent carnation growers, who in an able article contends that he has proved these conditions necessary in the propagation of this, his specialty, if he would foster and preserve freedom of bloom*.

In many instances it is necessary to the trade of the grower, or the wants of the locality where he may be, to raise a miscellaneous stock. On such a place it will

---

*American Florist, Vol. 8, page 236.

STOCK FOR PLANTING.

usually be found that every nook and corner is filled with market plants at the season of the year when the roses, upon which he must depend for his next winter's bloom, need both room and careful attention, precluding the possibility of his giving them the care and watchfulness necessary to have them in perfect form when needed for planting. Many growers so situated have given up trying to raise their own flowering stock, being satisfied that it is to their interest to contract with some specialist for their supply, giving him time to grow their plants so that they may be delivered at a specified time, and in size and condition superior to what his limited facilities would permit.

We hear of "two-eyed cuttings," and see plants advertised as having been grown from such. The supposition is that there is an eye at either end of the cutting, one of which is placed in the sand and around which the roots form, while the other constitutes the nucleus of the future plant. Unless it is desired to have roses send up canes from the base, or from underneath the surface soil, it is a mistake to insert an eye in the sand, or to leave a heel on the cutting, as that is full of eyes. Such canes almost invariably throw a cluster of buds, and are deficient in length of stem and foliage. Every encouragement should be given to have the plants break from their heads, throwing long stems, terminated by single buds, and thus be enabled to give both the length of stem and luxuriance of foliage so much in demand. If it is desired to produce plants quickly several eyes may be left above the sand; otherwise I know of no advantage gained by the use of more than one eye to a cutting, provided, always, that the stem of the cutting is of sufficient length to maintain itself in the sand until rooted.

American Beauty is an exception to the rule of one-eyed cuttings, because it is so closely jointed it is often necessary to use several eyes in order to obtain a cutting of sufficient length. It is also desirable to encourage this variety to break from the base, and to this end it is well to place one or more eyes in the sand.

It is customary with some to grow their plants to a good size in four-inch pots, and then rest them for two weeks before planting. This is done by plunging the pots outside, or setting them on a bed of coal ashes, withholding water in a measure, until the wood is well ripened, and I have seen them sometimes so thoroughly ripened that the foliage assumed a yellowish tint as though autumn had really overtaken them. I have never been able to see any beneficial results from this method, and prefer planting permanently without any rest after reaching this stage of growth.

From the time the cutting is placed in the sand until it is thrown out as an exhausted plant the following season, I do not believe it should receive a check of any kind, but on the contrary, that every possible means should be employed to keep it in a healthful vigorous growth, and the later the planting is done, the more advanced and vigorous should the pot plants be.

The question naturally arises, will not this impair the constitutional vigor of our stock? I am aware that at least two extensive growers of the rose so contend. They advocate an occasional outside planting of a year's stock, giving it a summer's growth in the open ground, a natural rest in winter, then starting it into growth early in the spring and from the wood thus grown, make the stock for flowering.

If it is found to be necessary, this is a rational way of restoring impaired vitality, but being an expensive method, should be avoided if others more inexpensive can be found which will accomplish the same result, and I think an occasional renewal of stock through the use of semi-dormant cuttings made in the fall, and rooted cool, a better, as well as a less expensive method.

When cuttings are first potted, they should be screened from bright sunshine until root action begins. Ever after this stage until planted, give the young plants the benefit of the best bench in the house under full sunlight. Carefully observe all the conditions of syringing, airing and shifting, necessary to a perfectly healthy stocky growth, and I do not think you need fear any deterioration in the constitutional vigor of your roses.

When roses are planted carelessly, left to the care of incompetent help, the temperature allowed to run up to 100° more or less before ventilation is given, and drop to 40 or 50 at night while the fireman enjoys a quiet nap, you can certainly look for impaired vitality.

If you have a healthy child, will you keep him in a close, unventilated room at a high temperature for fear a breath of air will subject him to a cold and its attendant evils, or will you follow your physician's advice—clothe him warmly and send him out into the air and sunshine, to romp on the lawn or roll in the sand as suits his inclination, taking care at the same time to supply him liberally with the Scotchman's diet? Then, so far as these principles accord with common sense and experience, apply them to plant life and you will find healthy, sturdy, vigorous growth your reward.

It is mistaken economy when obliged to defer planting later than July, to use anything but the best and strongest of stock; in fact, there is *no* economy in using or buying plants for this purpose because they are cheap. Whether you raise your own, or whether you buy of others, never use or buy any but the best, and for such, if obliged to purchase, be willing to pay the grower a fair compensation.

CHAPTER XIII.
THE RENEWAL OF ROSE PLANTS.

It will have been noticed that I have assumed that all planting was to be renewed each year. I sincerely wish I could advise flowering them the second season, especially such as are not overgrown and exhausted; it would save so much time and expense.

Sometimes, owing to a delay in planting, a bench does not arrive at its best until March or April, and as we look it over, note the size and number of the buds, as well as the fine thrifty foliage, we persuade ourselves easily, that *this* bench will certainly do well another season. So I have thought several times, although previous experience had taught me better.

Two years since I allowed inclination to get the better of judgment, and a house of Mermets answering the description just given, were flowered the second season, or rather, an attempt was made in that direction. They were carefully summered, not being allowed to become dry enough to injure the fibrous roots as we thought. In the fall they were pruned, tied, as much of the soil as possible removed without injuring the roots, fresh soil and composted mulching applied, and they started slowly into growth.

The result was less than half a crop, and in March they were thrown out, making a net loss for that bit of experience of $500. This was on an ordinary raised bench.

Early last summer I prepared a solid bed, drained it well and transferred to it some one year old Beauties from a raised bench. They were fine plants, had not been overworked, and in moving them we first cut all around the plant, then taking them one by one, with a shovel removed them with as little disturbance to the roots as possible. Root growth was encouraged in these at once, and although they gave excellent promise and made a fair growth, less than one-half as many buds have been cut from it, as from the bench from which they were taken, which was replanted in June with young plants propagated early in March.

I know men who have in a few instances had fair success in growing roses in shallow benches the second year. But they are experts, and I notice do not try it if they have plenty of nice young plants to use instead.

As a rule, it is not the expert grower who tries this method. It is the novice to whom it seems not only a sacrifice of money, but of product as well, to throw the stock out and start anew.

I have two establishments in mind, both large, and they are illustrations of these two methods. One discarded all his stock, planted early with fresh young plants, and now at the close of the year, the growth is a marvel of beauty, and the product unexcelled. Four-fifths of the plants on the other place were retained, and the spectacle is as much of a marvel, in its way, as the first. Could photographic views of these living illustrations of our subject matter be placed before you side by side in these pages, I think it would forever cure any one of following in the footsteps of the " economical " man.

CHAPTER XIV.

ROSES IN SUMMER.

Those having a summer trade in cut flowers can raise a better class of flowers, and at the same time bridge over the gap made each season in the supply through the renewal of the benches, by having a few houses devoted to this special purpose.

Oftentimes during the summer there is a scarcity of first class cut blooms. For this various reasons exist. In many instances the plants have been allowed to become exhausted through lack of nourishment at the proper time. Others may have had their vitality impaired through inattention and consequent inroads of insects which sap their life. Plants, too, that have been handled well, and made to produce to their utmost for six months, are not in a condition to do as successful work during the warm months. They have been constantly pushing up towards the light, and now as the weather becomes warmer, the rank growth is too near the glass to produce buds of fine form and size. Added to these reasons is the fact that buds from newly planted stock are not, until the approach of cool weather, as firm nor as large as the market requires.

This want can be supplied by planting in solid beds and allowing them to come in and go out with the season. They should be housed to protect them from winds and storms, as well as the various insects which mar both flower and foliage on plants in the open ground. These houses should be so arranged as to keep out severe frosts, heat being supplied in sufficient quantity to keep them at from thirty to thirty-five during the winter months. With the turn of the season—usually in February—they can be pruned back, tied down if need be, mulched and brought gradually on, so that by the time the winter plants commence to fail, you will have a succession of sturdy bloom.

As fall approaches, leave the houses open to the weather until frost, letting nature ripen them in her own way and prepare them for their winter's rest.

The varieties to be selected for this work are such as observation teaches us need a warm summer temperature to bring them to perfection. There are many varieties, grand for summer flowering, that are utterly worthless in winter, and the reverse is equally true. It is useless to expect fine blooms in summer from plants which require a low temperature to bring them to perfection in winter. For instance, Mermet, Bride, or any other rose requiring the same temperature as these, is valueless in a high temperature. On the contrary, there are many varieties that need just such a temperature to bring out their greatest beauty. For a yellow, Etoile de Lyon is a fine summer rose, and still I doubt whether it will suit the buyer in all respects as well as Perle. In pink, both La France and Duchess of Albany are grand, and if we desire the more delicate shades, Mad. Pierre Guillott and Grace Darling will supply the want. For white, Marie Guillott is the best, unless it be Niphetos, but the latter, if on its own roots, is not strong enough for this purpose. If you will plant a house to a few Chromotella, say one every twenty feet, train them to cover an entire bench, budding the branches with Niphetos from time to time as they fill the space, you will in a few years have a wonderfully productive house of the very best of white roses.

Red can be supplied by the use of Meteor, which revels in a high temperature. There are still others, and they are favorites with all rose lovers, but this list gives a good range of color and others can be added according to the taste of the grower.

A system like this enables one to commence planting for winter bloom in season to have his plants at their best during the time when flowers are wanted most, and give the greatest returns.

CHAPTER XV.

DEPTH OF SOIL FOR PLANTING.

There is but little diversity of opinion to-day, among men of experience, as to the advisability of using shallow benches, instead of solid beds for winter flowering. In the early days of forcing, solid beds were in general use, and it was not until the necessity arose of devising some means for the extermination of the rose bug, or "little joker," as it is sometimes called, that the discovery was made that roses planted on shallow benches were more easily controlled, and could be made much more profitable even when renewed every season, than the uncertain, slow moving bushes whose roots take such deep hold of the soil as to make them in a measure beyond control, and hence uncertain for early forcing. We must remember that we are in a measure, reversing one of Nature's laws, and coaxing plants to bloom at a season of the year when it is natural for them to rest. This can only be done successfully when we are able to control root action, and this is accomplished by means of the shallow bench. As to the depth of soil to be used, authorities vary. Some say two and one-half inches, some three, others six and more. The objections to benches as fleet as those first mentioned are two. First, the roses must be planted while small in order to be able to cover the ball. This necessitates planting earlier than it is often advisable to remove the bearing crop, if sufficient time is to be given the new plants in which to make the growth they should before their season of flowering commences.

The other objection lies in the fact that during the heated term, when air must be given day and night, and in quantity, evaporation is so rapid as to endanger root action unless the utmost vigilance is exercised. To be sure, constant watchfulness is the key to success, but it is not advisable for one to double his responsibility in this respect, and as I believe, unnecessarily.

It is my custom, as a rule, to commence planting in May, selecting for this early work such benches as are paying the least. The plants used during this month and next are usually from three-inch pots, but all planting after June is, as a rule, from four-inch pots. This necessitates a depth of about five inches of soil in order to cover the ball well, and I am satisfied this depth is better than either more or less, if for a year's work.

CHAPTER XVI.
PLANTING.

To secure perfect drainage and thus keep the soil sweet, the benches should be constructed of boards not more than six inches wide, with a crack of half an inch between them.

When sod can be had in abundance it is well to cover the cracks in the bottom of the bench with it, putting the grass side down. This should be of uniform thickness, and as thin as it will hold together and permit of handling. The spade is too slow for this work, and every place of any size should possess a sod cutter where much is to be used. In case sod cannot be obtained, cover with clean straw, or with that which can be shaken out from the stable waste. Bring in your prepared soil and fill the bench. Level and firm the soil well, either by treading it with the feet or by tamping it with a brick, being careful to observe that there are no loose spots in the corners or around the edges. Many growers plant so those in the second row will be half way between those of the first, and so continue with each row, claiming for this method the advantage of each plant occupying an equal amount of space. See Fig. 21

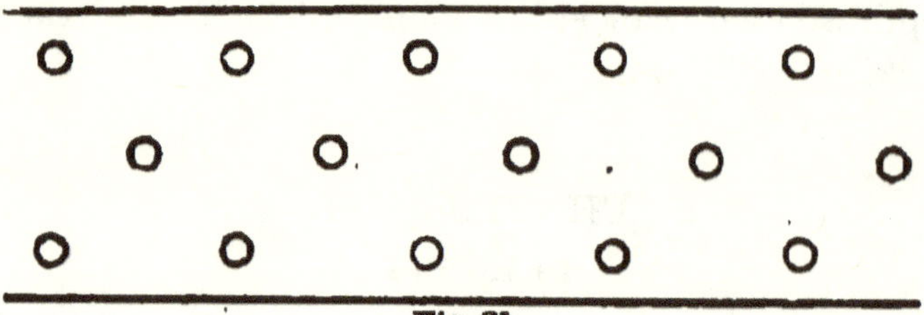

Fig. 21.

This is correct, but beds are more easily cared for when the rows run at right angles with each other, the first plan necessitating a walk through a centre bench.

When planting at right angles, in a bench eight feet wide plant seven rows. This will give twelve inches between the plants one way, and allow the two outside rows to be six inches from the edge of the bench. Fifteen inches, at least, should be the distance between the short rows across the bench. Some plant them as far as eighteen inches apart.

Planting should be done with accuracy, in order that each plant may have its exact amount of space. This will be rendered easy of accomplishment if the ends of the bench are spaced off, nails driven and a line stretched the whole length of the bench, the short rows across the bench having been previously marked out. Start with your middle row, and with a trowel cut out enough to receive the ball of the plant, letting its top be a little below the surface of the soil. Firm the soil well around the plant, leaving a slight depression where planted, for the better retention of water. Should your plants be uneven in size, assort them so that the strongest will be at the back or north row of the middle bench and the shortest in front, grading the bed with the slope of the roof. Care should be taken not to plant a dry ball. If such are found, dip in water until thoroughly soaked before planting.

If the side benches are of equal width, or three feet each, three rows can be planted on each of them, making a house one hundred feet by eighteen, to hold about 1,000 plants.

If the soil was in what is termed "a good growing condition" when placed in the bench, let your watering be light for a few days, filling the depression spoken of around the plant the first time water is applied, but confining its use to frequent light syringing until root action commences. In this way the roots will seek the surrounding soil much more rapidly than if the entire bench is water soaked.

In about ten days the surface will be covered with a multitude of small weeds. To exterminate these, on a bright sunny day, take a small fine rake and go over the whole carefully. If this is practiced every week for three or four weeks, there will be no necessity for hand picking, and by that time, the plants if strong at first, will have put out a vigorous growth and be ready for their first mulching, but to facilitate this they should be properly staked and tied.

CHAPTER XVII.
STAKING AND TYING.

I am not sure whether the old practice of cutting bean poles for the purpose of staking, in order to save buying canes, has been entirely abandoned or not. If not it should be, as it is a case of mistaken economy, for after filling the soil with timber and shading the plants with miniature forest trees, the poor roses have a hard struggle for their share of room and sunshine.

STAKING AND TYING.

Cane stakes from the Ohio river bottoms have been extensively used for this purpose, but are objectionable for several reasons. First, the lack of depth of soil will not permit any stake to enter a sufficient distance to stand erect without support. Second, such portion of it as enters the soil must be removed the following season, and one or two repetitions of this so shortens the stake as to render a new supply necessary. Third, being hollow they make an excellent harbor for insects, some of which if they obtain a foothold, will nest and live there, and be on hand at an early date to sample the new crop.

A better, though at first more expensive way, is to use galvanized wire. This requires two sizes, number six for the standards, and number sixteen for staying their tops and holding them in place. At either end of the bench place frames for the reception of the small wire. These can be constructed of gas pipe, or of wood as preferred. The horizontal part to which the wires are fastened, should be about three and one-half feet above the soil, or the top of it a few inches below the purlin. Brace these frames well either in front, or by attaching strong wires, one end of which has been fastened to the end of the house, so that the tension will not spring the frame. Take an end of the wire, double and make a twist about ten inches long, pass this around the pipe or through a staple as the case may be, and fasten securely by neatly winding one-half of the twisted piece around the other. This will give it greater strength and render it more capable of withstanding the tension. With a wire stretcher draw the wire taut, double and fasten around the frame at the other end of the bench in the same way as the first. Continue in this manner until all your upper wires are in position, being careful to draw all of them equally taut.

The number required will depend upon the number of plants. If there are seven across the bench, it will require sixteen stakes, or two to a plant, and the same number of small wires for their support.

Before stretching the first wire, mark each end of the frame so that the spaces between the wires will be equal, and after they are all in position they can be staid in the following manner: Arrange the supports to both the ridge and purlin so that at every twenty or twenty-five feet they shall be opposite each other, and at right angles to the bench. To these fasten at each end a strip two inches by half an inch, into one edge of which a saw calf has been made a quarter of an inch deep, and of a size and corresponding distance that will just receive the wires, and you will have a firm wire frame to work to. This should all be in place before the bed is planted.

If it is your custom to bring in and carry out the soil in hand flats, the wire frame over the middle bench can be made permanent, but if wheelbarrows or hand

STAKING AND TYING. 69

carts are used, necessitating travel back and forth on the bench, the frames can with little trouble be so constructed as to admit of the wire frame being raised on the north side nearly to the glass and thus be out of the way. To do this, if it is desired to construct the

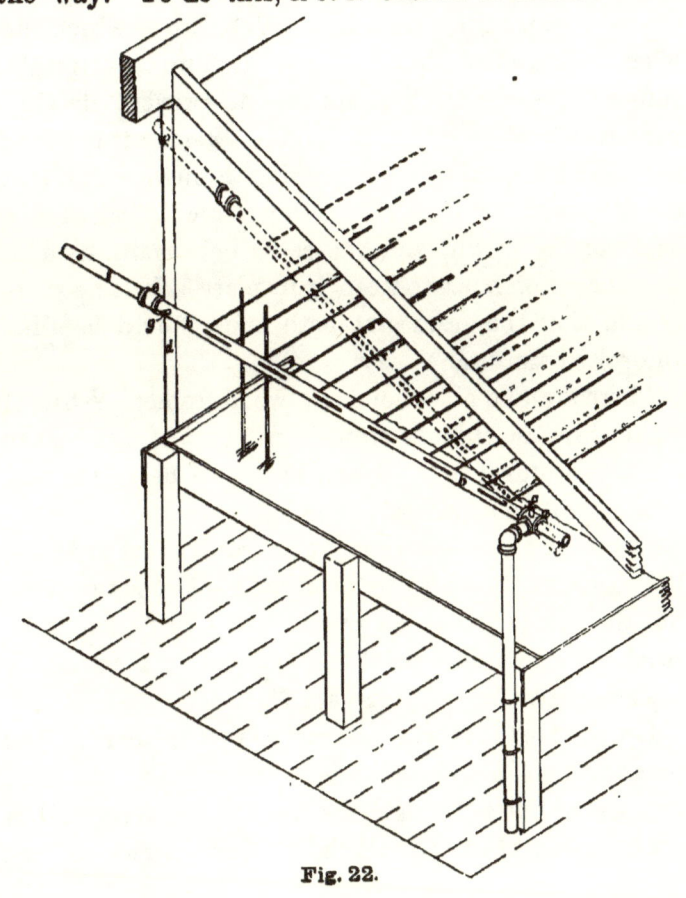

Fig. 22.

frame of wood, use four by four oak or some other firm wood, join one end of the horizontal bar to the shorter upright by means of a bolt passing through both, and thus form a flexible joint.

Let the longer upright extend as far as it will be desirable to raise the wire frame. The bar to which the wires are attached should extend beyond this upright sufficiently—about eight inches—to prevent its slipping inside when raised to its top. Fasten this bar at the height desired by a bolt passing through both it and the standard, so that when the frame is raised the bolt can be drawn, and the same bolt again used in another set of holes to keep it in place. It is needless to add that the frames at both ends should be alike and raised simultaneously.

There are two objections to a wood frame. While it is the cheapest, it looks clumsy, and projecting over the walk, as a movable one must, is apt to be in the way when one is thoughtlessly passing.

In order to construct a movable frame of gas pipe, the bar to which the wires are attached should be two-inch, but the uprights may be of one and a half inch if desired. For making the flexible joint, use an ell, or a close nip and a tee. See Fig 22.

Let the tee (a) be rimmed out so that the bar (b) will pass through it, and drill a hole for a pin (c), also drill two sets of holes through the bar for the reception of the pin (c), these should be at right angles to each

STAKING AND TYING.

other, or in other words, by them divide the circumference of the bar into four spaces of equal distance.

Instead of letting the bar project beyond the long standard (d), cap it with a coupling (e) that will project but an inch, and when it is desired to raise the frame, a short piece of pipe (f) can be screwed into the coupling, and provision can be made for fastening both this and the main bar, by drilling holes in both them and the post, that will admit a bolt (g) of suitable size to hold them in place. These frames should be held firmly in place by strong wires fastened securely to the ends of the house.

Before staking in the fall, if the wires have become slack, place a pair of tongs on each end of the bar (b), remove pins (c) and (g) and turn the bar until the wires are taut, then fasten as before.

The upright wires should be cut at the factory into suitable lengths. For a middle bench of ordinary height the first four rows on the south side should be four feet in length, the balance six inches longer. Those four feet long can also be used on the north bench.

On a south bench overhead wires will not be necessary, and they had better be put in permanently on the north bench.

In staking, wires are inserted about three inches in the soil and the same distance each way from the plant, and then tied to the top wires, care being taken to keep them in exact line and even at the top. This system of tying permits of spreading the plant so that all the space may be occupied, and still not have the foliage bunched, a great assistance in syringing thoroughly. It also leaves space between the rows for the free admission of both air and sunlight, not only to the plants, but to the soil as well.

The cost of fitting up a house one hundred by eighteen feet in this way, exclusive of labor, is about twenty-five dollars, but it has to be done but once, and possesses so many advantages that no one after trying it will regret the outlay.

CHAPTER XVIII.
MULCHING.

The roses being staked and tied, are now ready for mulching. This should be composed of two-thirds well rotted cow manure, and one-third good soil. If the manure is two years old, all the better. Mix well and apply about an inch deep all over the surface. From this time on the soil should never be disturbed, as the plants will throw up a multitude of new roots to absorb this covering, and any weeds that appear after this should be carefully removed by hand.

If all goes well, the earlier beds may be mulched again in seven or eight weeks, using, if the first is well spent, a little more, and it can also be made a little stronger now by the addition of a gallon of bone meal to a cubic yard of mulch. If the weather is bright and clear and the plants in perfect health, an inch and a half may be applied, but if from any cause, known or unknown, the plants seem sickly, they are in no better condition to absorb strong food than are either men or animals under the same conditions, and it should be withheld until such time as root action is better.

As a rule, it is not well to mulch heavily in November or December, but on bright days during these months, if you are satisfied more nourishment is needed and that the plants are in a condition to receive it, a very small amount of fresher manure may be scattered very lightly here and there between the rows, allowing the same to be washed in from time to time as the plants are either watered or syringed. This is quicker than to apply food in liquid form, where but little can be used. I am no advocate of the use of green manure in quantity for this purpose at this season of the year. Besides being offensive, it is dangerous in the hands of any but experts, but during the months mentioned, when a heavy mulch cannot be safely applied, used very sparingly, it often helps sustain the plants until the dull cold months are passed.

Another and heavier coat than the second one may usually be added by February, and this will be the last to be applied to such benches as are to be used for the first planting for another season's work. Or if the plants are healthy and the soil full of working roots, liquid manure may be used quite freely.

In addition to these applications, it will under some conditions be found advisable to use nitrate of soda in small quantity after the buds are formed and just before maturing.

Used thus, if the mulching has been on for some time, it will materially aid the bud to develop size, but its use at other times is inadvisable, because it tends to make a rapid soft growth, which in some varieties lessens productiveness.

CHAPTER XIX.
WATERING.

Watering and ventilating are no doubt the rocks on which many a man's hopes have been wrecked. Everything went beautifully as long as the sun shone brightly, but when November came with its grey, leaden sky, followed by December with its piercing cold, its storms, covering what of the glass frosts had not claimed, somehow, the plants seemed to grow less day by day, instead of pushing on vigorously as they had during the summer and early fall. One day's mistake at this critical period, and your summer's work goes for naught.

No set rules can be either laid down or followed in

regard to watering. It is largely a matter of intuition. A nameless something, that comes to the individual only through close observation and careful study, and then only as he develops daily an aptitude for grasping the situation. I have known those who performed this important work by rule. Every morning at just such an hour, cold or hot, wet or dry, syringing was done, and to save early firing as fall weather came on, all ventilation was closed early in the afternoon. It is unnecessary to add that these methods were not productive of pecuniary success. Even now, as I write (December 15th), a letter of inquiry reaches me from a beginner wishing to know why the outer petals cling and decay on the buds in his house. A question easy of solution without seeing the conditions. Either too much water or too little air, or both combined and administered injudiciously.

One finds pen and ink to be poor and imperfect mediums through which to convey to another the elements of success in this most difficult part of the work attending artificial growth. I wish I could describe it, but it is beyond the power of pen or tongue. It is like the blind girl yearning for knowledge. Her delicate touch brings her in contact with form, and that form imparts to her mind language in embryo, until by the most persistent effort, and constant watchfulness, words, sentences, language, is at her command. So in this. To the delicate touch and watchful eye it comes as by intuition, and I cannot tell you better how a man comes into possession of this art, for art it is if ever there was one. Only general principles can be outlined. The application of them to existing circumstances must be largely at the discretion of the operator.

During the summer and fall, the soil should be kept in a good growing condition, not dry, neither should it be saturated, for it must be remembered the soil is far from being filled with working roots, and in their absence moisture cannot be as readily taken up as in the spring when these conditions are different. Examine carefully every bed each day and determine what it needs. If the soil has a "growing touch," if you can close the hand upon it and upon opening have the soil retain its form as though it had been cast in a mould, syringe only, letting the quantity of water used be governed by the character of the day. Never let your soil get in such a condition that you can squeeze water from it, not even a drop. This applies, of course, only to a soil that has become sodden from too much water, not to one recently watered. Occasionally let the benches get a little dry, then on a bright day water well, remembering always, the more dense the foliage, and the more the plants are bearing, the greater will be the amount of moisture they will need and absorb. On every bright day the foliage should be well syringed. This should be done early in the day in order that it may have sufficient time to dry should it become cloudy later on. If possible to avoid it, night should never find any dampness on the foliage, especially after the days begin to shorten and the nights to grow cool.

As winter approaches, more care still must be exercised, and if the day is dull, or moist, use no water unless careful examination reveals dry spots in the soil, and then sparingly. In a clear, bright winter day, examine all the benches thoroughly, giving to each in proportion to its need. Also use every opportunity when the sun is bright and the glass clear of snow and frost, to syringe well. If you succeed in tiding over the winter months and keep your roses in a healthy growing condition, as the sun grows stronger and the soil becomes full of roots, the quantity must be increased, and after the middle of February there is but little danger of giving them too much on bright, airy days.

CHAPTER XX.
VENTILATION.

It is a difficult matter to say which of the two, this or the former, constitutes the key stone upon which success depends. Certain it is they go hand in hand and require equally intelligent action.

From the day the houses are planted until the roses are thrown out as worthless, all the air possible should be given.

Not that every day in this respect is like the one that preceded it, in which the same treatment is required, but the days are rare that ventilation in some form cannot be given.

It must be borne in mind constantly that the health and vigor of your plants, and that their ability to afford you remuneration during the winter, is largely dependent upon the growth they make previous to November. If the heat is extreme, throw wide open every ventilator, and these are the days when you reap the benefit of having a house stand by itself, with nothing joined to it to radiate heat or impede a free circulation of air through the doors in the walls. These ventilators should be shut at night unless the temperature is extremely high, and gives indications of continuing so through the night, but as long as possible leave roof ventilation open night and day.

Also in seasons of extreme heat, while syringing freely, be careful not to saturate the soil, as it tends to soften and enfeeble the growth.

As fall approaches, gradually lessen the amount of air at night, tempering it to the weather, but still leaving on all that the plants will bear without engendering mildew. If the wind is raw, shut the ventilators on the side from which it comes, keeping the other side open, but not allowing strong drafts of cool air to blow directly on the plants.

Some times as early as August a cold rain will set in

VENTILATION.

for a day or two, and although the thermometer may not fall below sixty, the change from summer heat is very great. Whenever this occurs, no matter if it is in July, start a little circulation in your pipes, leaving the ventilators open sufficiently to prevent the temperature from rising unduly, and this will allow gathered moisture to escape.

The great aim to be sought after is an even temperature, and as often as the changes of the season rise above or fall below our standard, just so often must we employ every means in our power to counteract their extremes.

The habit of closing the ventilators to save fuel, or the trouble of starting the fires, as well as the idea that no fire is needed until frosts come, has not yet wholly passed out of practice or belief, and it may truly be said to be the lazy man's economy. Not a season passes but what, somewhere, I enter just such houses as these. Could their owners but know that for every dollar saved in this way they were drawing on the future for ten, and perhaps hundreds of dollars, they would, if they desired to consult their own best interest, reverse the practice.

Should the day be bright and warm and the night following so cool as to cause the thermometer to fall to 50 or 55, you will find in the morning that the foliage is covered with dew. To the novice this may seem a healthy condition, but a few nights of this, and in a short time the leaves will begin to fall, the young red shoots will take on a "water logged," purplish hue, and the plants will have received a check from which they will not recover until spring, and it will require the utmost skill to bring them through alive.

I feel that too much stress cannot be laid upon this point, for the evil described is but one of several that arise from the same cause. Never leave your houses without starting a fire, if you are satisfied the night temperature will fall much below 60, leaving on at the same time a little air, the amount of which must be governed by the outside temperature.

As soon as the weather becomes cool enough to close the ventilators nights, every bright morning, as soon as the sun strikes the glass, open one side a little. In a half hour open another notch. Watch the day, the winds and the outside temperature, as well as that in the house, and continue to give more as the day advances. If the sun enters a cloud for any length of time and the air outside is keen, lower your ventilators in proportion until the sun appears again. Should the wind change and blow into the house, close that side and open the other at once. Do not think when you have once opened the ventilators your work for the day is over. During the winter months, scarcely an hour will pass in which some change is not required, and ever remember that eternal vigilance is the price at which a paying crop is grown.

CHAPTER XXI.

TEMPERATURE OF WATER.

Bob Burdette says the man who wrote so charmingly of the invigorating and healthful results attending the practice of rising early, taking a bath in ice water, a brisk walk and then breakfasting, drew entirely upon his imagination for this unpopular advice; that, in fact, the author theorized for the benefit of others while snugly ensconced in a warm bed, which he did not, as a rule, leave until eleven o'clock in the morning.

While "cleanliness is next to godliness," let us have it tempered a little—that is, the water—not only for ourselves, but vegetation as well. A greater crank even than Thompson would he be considered who advocated deluging tender plants with ice water. To be sure they cannot resist and must meekly take whatever their master provides, but the evil results will be seen later on.

The importance of this is such that there should be facilities of some kind provided on every place to bring water to a proper degree of warmth before applying it to either root or foliage. I have seen roses syringed on a bright day with extremely cold water with this result. An examination soon revealed multitudes of small mildew blisters all over the surface of the leaves, from the size of a pin head down, until they could not be seen by the naked eye. Vegetable pneumonia, that is what it was. Leaves are the lungs of the plant. When they become diseased you have a case of vegetable consumption on your hands.

Quite a majority of the larger growers are located outside of cities, and are thus obliged to provide water works of their own. To obtain the required pressure it is customary to raise the water to tanks varying in height from fifteen to twenty-five feet. This renders it comparatively easy to so arrange as to be able to keep the water at an even and desired temperature. If convenient to do so, a separate flow and return can be provided between the boiler and tank, or if steam heating is used, a coil of pipe in the tank can be used. The use of a coil will be found the more agreeable way, turning the end of the coil so the steam, after passing through it, shall be discharged near the bottom of the tank, as the noise from turning a jet of steam directly into the water is objectionable. If the coil is of sufficient length, the heat will all be absorbed before the jet reaches the discharge, and all noise thus be avoided.

If your boiler is not able to do this extra work, by all means provide a special one for the purpose. For this, a hot water heater of some kind will require the least attention, being very easily regulated. The arrangement is the most simple possible. After setting the boiler, presumably in the enclosure under the tank, attach the flow and return to the bottom of whatever contains your water supply, and it is ready for use. For this purpose a boiler costing $25 will be found to be of sufficient capacity to temper 300 barrels of water.

To temper a supply from city hydrants so that it shall be even, is not so easy a matter, unless it be done in a similar way. This would require a receptacle for the water sufficiently strong to resist the pressure, but will, I think, be more satisfactory than other methods if a considerable quantity of water is needed. Whenever the construction is such as has just been described, after the water has been brought to the required temperature, shut off the pressure while using, depending upon the elevation to give what is needed. In this way all used will be of even temperature, while if you draw out and allow the high hydrant pressure to fill at the same time, there will necessarily be more or less variation in the degree of warmth in the water used. This is the objection, as it seems to me, to the plan advocated by some, of having a hollow saddle back boiler set over a row of pipes under a bench, filling it with water, attaching the hydrant to one end and drawing from the other, dependence being made upon the pipes under it for tempering. Some depend upon having a sufficient number of water pipes in the house to temper the water used for syringing, but if much is needed the supply soon becomes exhausted.

I know of no better way for winter work than that first described, whether the water supply be public or private.

While there is not as much danger in the use of warm as of cold water, if applied to the roots it should be some cooler than the atmosphere of the house. If warmer than 50 or 55, it will have a tendency to encourage a more rapid growth than is advisable, but water of the same temperature as the house can be safely used in syringing, when the application is light.

CHAPTER XXII.
SHADING.

The necessity for this varies with the locality and the season. In early spring, as the days become warmer, if the plants have grown well, they will be throwing their buds near the glass. Bright sunshine on the clear glass at this time will not only bleach the color but hasten the maturity of the buds, thus lessening their size. It is best under these circumstances to apply a very light shade, just enough to break the glare of the sun. For this a thin wash may be made by putting a small amount of white lead in the quantity of refined coal oil necessary to go over the surface required. This can be applied evenly as well as quite rapidly, by means of a whitewash brush, having a handle of sufficient length to reach the highest point to be covered. I am not in sympathy with those who advocate the application of shading with a syringe, "because it saves time." What is worth doing at all is worth doing well, and while in northern latitudes it may be best to apply it in the form of a fine spray, thus leaving both shade and clear glass, in the latitude in which this is written it is not the best method. I would never, if possible to avoid it, use whitewash. The lime will not only destroy the paint, but eat the oil from the putty, loosening and causing it to separate from the wood long before the elements will naturally require the roof to be newly glazed. If it is desired to make a preparation that will wash off easily or disappear with the first rain, water colored with a little clay will accomplish the purpose, leaving no injurious effects behind.

Another piece of false economy is to shade heavily in order not to be obliged to devote time to it again during the season. Shade lightly, and with reference to the time and crop to be protected, and if it is needed again during the season, apply as, when and where it seems necessary. This cry about making work is nonsense. Muscle is cheap; it is brain that comes high. I would not advocate unnecessary work, and this is not; it is directly in the line of what we are striving for, the best results first, labor saving and devices for its accomplishment, second.

I have visited establishments where the shading has been so thorough that the plants resented it and strove to overcome the lack of light by climbing rapidly upward in hopes of being able to walk out into God's sunshine. The result was what must always be expected under like conditions, long spaced joints, spindling growth, impaired vigor. Splendid subjects for black spot, falling leaves, disappointed hopes.

CHAPTER XXIII.
THE CUTTING OF BUDS.

The stage at which this should be done depends upon the use to which it is desired to put the flowers. If you are near your market and they are for immediate sale over the counter, they will need to be more advanced than if they are for shipment to some distant point. It has been proved that roses will both show and keep better, not to be offered for sale the same day they are cut, but be kept in water from twelve to twenty-four hours, according to the varieties.

The work of sorting, packing and getting the product to market, consumes the morning hours, and usually needs to be performed, in cool weather, before the day is sufficiently advanced, to gather such as have developed during the night. Experience and careful watchfulness will enable one to form an accurate opinion as to the amount a bud will develop between the hour it is cut, and the time it is to be placed on the market. For this reason the cutting of buds is work the proprietor should either do himself or train some trusty young man to have charge of, and if possible it should be done by one or two men, giving each charge of a section to which their personal attention is given, and for the care of which they are responsible. In this way every bush and every bud is known to the person in charge, and he will soon be able to keep them in mind and tell very nearly the hour in which they will need to be gathered, thus avoiding a useless expenditure of time watching them, and loss as well from overdevelopment.

No more should be cut in the morning than are ready, and the stems of these should be put in fresh cool water, and placed where they are to be kept without any unnecessary delay, and they should be gathered in the same manner throughout the day whenever they are matured. If the morning gathering is more than can be attended to by those in charge after working hours commence, either train others to assist or have this work commenced earlier in the day, giving those who perform it an equal amount of time at its close. If your helpers are permanently located with you, this will be found to be the most satisfactory system. If they are not, you must have others in training to fill their place when they step out. This is not the only kind of work that cannot be performed by fixed rules, but perfect system must be mantained if we would make the most of our opportunities.

Buds for distant shipment need to be cut closer than those for home use. This must also be performed upon the judgment of the operator. Time, distance, varieties, all have their bearing and must be considered, and while not demanding the close watchfulness of those cut for home use, they should be gathered at least three times on sunny days. This will bring them to maturity evenly, and the stems of those cut in the early part of the day will have absorbed water enough by evening to permit of their being forwarded to their destination.

The demand for long foliage is now such, there is little danger of so many joints being left as in time to make the plants unduly tall or "leggy," as it is sometimes expressed, but there is danger of cutting back too far. A new break will be formed and another bud mature soonest from a leaf about midway between the bud and the union of its stem to the main plant, but if this is practiced every time a bud is cut, the plants will soon reach the glass, and the amount of foliage accompanying the buds will be too small to satisfy the buyer. If cut back too far, the leaf remaining will be small and the new break slower in making its appearance, as well as less vigorous than it should be. For this reason a bud should not be severed without leaving two eyes, and three if the others are shown by small or undersized leaves. It is usually the case that the second leaf will throw a strong renewal of bud and foliage.

If underbrush accumulates and has passed its usefulness, remove it; also varieties inclined to make a quantity of blind wood should occasionally be gone over and enough of it pruned out to prevent its bunching and making it difficult to reach all parts of the foliage with a syringe. At the same time, it must be borne in mind the plant must have an abundance of foliage to breathe through, and that excessive trimming will impair its vitality if not destroy it altogether. This condition of things will sometimes be seen in American Beauty. This rose does not incline to make side shoots as do many others, and will oftentimes throw several canes which come to maturity at about the same time. If these are all cut back sharp in order to obtain the length of stem which establishes their value, the plant is nearly robbed of its foliage, and unless water has been and is withheld at once, and the plant allowed to become somewhat dry for a short time, the fibrous roots will cease to act, the foliage left will turn yellow, the plant sicken and rarely recover in season to be of further use.

As before mentioned, the cutting should be done by the proprietor or his foreman, whenever practicable; if not, then under their personal supervision, as it is of great importance that it be performed at the right time and in the right way. This daily care also brings to one's attention constantly, all the conditions pertaining to success—ventilation, watering, syringing, etc. It gives also opportunity for watchfulness, and if the person is quick to observe, this experience will soon make him as much of an adept in all that pertains to the health and life of plants as is the physician who studies the health of his patient.

CHAPTER XXIV.
GRADING AND PACKING.

In making up your shipment, whether for home or abroad, carefully assort them into two or three grades, as will best suit those to whom you sell, and you will usually find the first grade will sell, even if the market is dull, while those sent in by your less particular neighbor, unsorted, will often be seen at night where they were placed in the morning. It is better to throw away all culls, short stems and imperfect flowers, than, by placing all together, so impair the quality that they must be sold for a less price, or, what is worse, not at all. I am now speaking of the wholesale trade, and if you would catch buyers you must avail yourself of every advantage to display your stock at its best. With this end in view, it is always best for short distance shipments, after grading, to pack each variety by itself, in long light wooden trays, one tier deep, and in such a way that each bud will show what it is. The advantage gained by displaying them in this manner will more than compensate for the cost of returning the empty trays, even if you are at the mercy of an express company.

Mixed colors shipped on special orders, should be packed in light wood boxes, with the foliage in the center. Between each layer put a strip of wax paper to keep them from bruising, and when finished, place a small piece of ice on the foliage, binding both it and the stems so there can be no motion, and consequent injury if the box is overturned.

CHAPTER XXV.
THE PRESERVATION OF FLOWERS.

The usual method of placing roses in an ice box in order to keep them, is a mistake, and it is worse than a mistake to "pickle" them for a prospective future demand.

My attention was once called to the fact that a pot of roses was placed in the unused ash pit of a cool cellar. This ash pit connected with an old-fashioned chimney, up which a strong draft constantly passed. These roses were forgotten for several days, but to the surprise of all who saw them, they were in perfect condition when found, and greatly superior in size to what they were when placed there.

This suggested to me that we might be pursuing a wrong practice in placing roses in a damp, cold box, from which all light was excluded, and that the accidental discovery just given was the true method. Subsequent trials proved this to be correct, and for some years I have discarded the use of ice as a preservative, except in cases of shipment, having prepared a cellar for their storage in the following manner:

Select a sheltered, shady location for a cellar, and if you do not wish to cover it with a packing room, let it be on the north side or end of some building, so that the sun will be excluded. Excavate to a sufficient depth, brick or wall up the sides, provide drainage if inclined to be damp, and lay a brick floor. Let the cellar project two feet beyond the end of the building, and over this place a roof of heavy glass, slanting the same sufficiently to shed any water that may fall upon it. Arrange a shutter over this that can be used or removed at will, giving light or excluding it in the brighter part of the day. Make a wooden flue, eight or ten inches square, and let one end of it be near the ceiling of the cellar, from which it should rise from ten to twenty-five feet, according to circumstances. Arrange the end that is in the cellar with a slide, so more or less of it can be utilized at will, and it will serve to carry off all dampness, keeping the air in the cellar clean and sweet.

It may be unnecessary to add that this should be kept scrupulously clean, and should not be used for general purposes.

The Preservation of Flowers.

Side ventilation should be provided by having one or more narrow windows. If shaded so the sun cannot strike it either morning or evening, it is well to have one on both the east and west sides. In the spring and fall these will be found very useful, as they can be thrown open in the early morning hour, before the sun changes the temperature, or they can be opened late in the evening and closed before sunrise, which will result in lowering the inside temperature several degrees, and if they are kept closed through the day it will rise but little. This will require early rising, and is not the method for the man who wants to save all the work possible, whether it conduces to success or not.

In the extreme heat of summer it may be found advisable to lower the temperature by the use of ice. This will not often occur, and when it is necessary, see that it is as far from the blooms as possible, as it tends to bleach all colored varieties.

As the roses are cut and brought in, they should be set on the floor under the skylight, and most varieties will be found to improve with this treatment, and the next day they will be found to be in much better condition for retail sale than when placed there.

It is a well-known fact in cities that the poor "fakir" who stores the flowers not desired for display under the sidewalk in some cool cellar, keeps his stock longer and in better condition than the tradesman who places them in high priced ice boxes. In the cooling cellar, pains should be taken to prevent the ingress of warm air. The entrance should be used as little as possible during a warm day.

CHAPTER XXVI.
INSECT ENEMIES.

From the day Adam found himself surrounded by "thorns and thistles," until the present time, it would

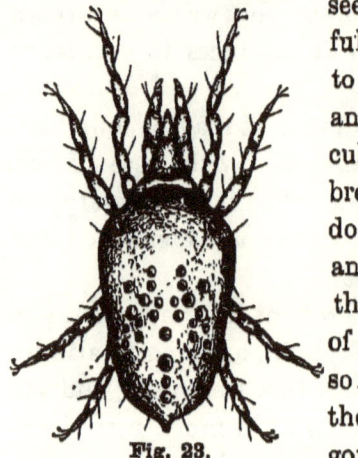

Fig. 23.

seem that everything beautiful in nature had an enemy to either mar or destroy it, and the higher the degree of cultivation to which they are brought, the more numerous do these pests seem to become, and the more malignant are their attacks. Insect enemies of all kinds have increased so rapidly of late, as to require the services of experts from government stations to investigate cause and cure, but not in all cases have they been able to point out the latter.

Red Spider is one of the most ancient as well as ever-present enemies of the rose. While very minute, it can easily be seen with the naked eye, and viewed under a microscope, we cease to wonder at its ravages, when left in undisputed possession for any length of time. See Fig. 23.

Their depredations will always be found to be on the under side of the leaves, and unless carefully watched for, their presence may not be known until the face of the leaf assumes a spotted ashen hue, caused by their having destroyed the tissue, and in such cases they will be found in considerable quantity and of all sizes. That they should never be allowed to gain a foothold, is the rule, but in practice it is not always accomplished.

They thrive and multiply rapidly in a dry, hot atmosphere, hence, from the time the cutting is made it should be the effort of the grower to prevent this condition. They cannot thrive in a moist atmosphere; for this reason it is desirable to frequently syringe lightly, during dry warm days, wetting, at the same time, all wood work of the benches, the walks and ground underneath, being careful always to give the spray full on the under side of the leaves. To do this effectually, it will be necessary to syringe from different sides alternately, and if the middle bench is wide enough for a narrow walk in the center, see that a small hose is taken through it occasionally, lest they find lodgment there. You may set him down as a careless workman who lets this enemy gain the ascendancy. If, from any cause, they do become too numerous to conquer in the usual way, to a bucket of water add a pint of very sharp vinegar and apply with a hand syringe to the under side of the leaves. An application every other day, for a week, will so reduce them in numbers, that at the expiration of that time a proper amount of syringing will keep them down.

Another troublesome pest is the Rose Bug. *Aramigus fullerii.* (Horn). This is supposed to have been imported from Europe some years since, and until its habits were studied and means taken to prevent its multiplying, was very destructive.

The beetle is about one-half the size of the illustration, of a very dark brown, almost black, color, and feeds upon the foliage. See Fig. 24. Its presence may be detected by small semi-circular pieces being taken from the edge of the leaves. It is extremely shy, remaining hid in some safe sheltered place on the plant during the day, seeking its food during the night. Hand picking, though slow and tedious, is a good way in which to become acquainted with its habits, but if much of a foothold has been obtained by them the quicker way is to spread white cloth under the plants, then giving the plant several sharp jars, by striking it with the hand, they will usually be dislodged and fall on the cloth, from which they may be gathered and destroyed. A careful, persistent course like this is the only way in which they can be exterminated where plants are

Fig. 24.

permanent and remain for years in the same soil. It is not the beetle, however, which destroys the plant, but its young while in the larva state, by feeding on the roots, and if they have been allowed to multiply undisturbed they soon become numerous enough to destroy whole benches. See Fig. 25. It is the habit of the

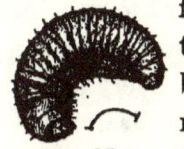

Fig. 25.

female beetle to deposit her eggs around the base of the plant, in crevices of the bark, or just under the soil. One writer recommends placing around the base of the plants a piece of cloth in which they will seek to hide their eggs. This being removed every two weeks, thoroughly scalded and replaced, will help to exterminate them. So troublesome were these pests in some localities a few years since, that solid benches were almost entirely given up. Shallow ones were substituted, and new soil and plants being used every year, so prevented their multiplying we now seldom hear of any one being troubled with them. They are fond of heliotrope, and old plants used for flowering from year to year are liable to become infested with them if they enter the houses.

When houses are thoroughly cleaned every year, and all soil and plants removed, there is nothing to fear from them, but it is well to be always on the watch where any kinds of plants are retained from year to year, as they have been known to attack other species in the absence of those they like best.

The Leaf Roller, though comparatively new under glass, is a great annoyance, and as yet no remedy has been discovered for it but hand picking. Its presence will be indicated by the rolling of a leaf, an examination of which reveals a worm about a half an inch in length, enveloped by a web around which the leaf rolls. These greatly disfigure the foliage if allowed to remain, and I am told some growers find it necessary to make a thorough and systematic search for them every morning. Protected as they are by both web and leaf, nothing in the way of liquids or fumes have any effect upon them.

At some seasons of the year an insect known as Thrip is more or less troublesome. Prof. Baker, of Michigan Agricultural College, to whom we are greatly indebted for the publicity he has given to his researches regarding the habits of injurious insects, says of this: "These belong to the family Thripidæ, the members of which may be recognized by the following characterestics: They have four long, narrow membranous wings which are fringed with long hairs and sometimes have one or two longitudinal veins; in repose the wings lie along the back. The mouth parts resemble somewhat those of biting insects, and somewhat those of sucking insects. The body is long and narrow, the head being somewhat narrower than the thorax. The compound eyes are large, and there are three simple eyes. Some forms are wingless, in this species the male being wingless. They

Insect Enemies.

are light yellow in color, very lively, being able to run and jump with great rapidity." See Fig. 26. There are several species of Thrips. Those troublesome to the rose belong to the genus Limothrips. These usually put in their appearance, if at all, late in the spring, after the weather becomes warm, and the plants more or less debilitated. They are very lively, disappearing quickly at the base of the petals, when disturbed, among which they work, and often render worthless before the buds mature enough to cut.

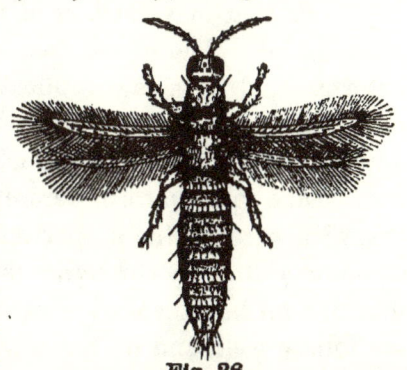

Fig. 26.

Protected as they are among the unopened petals, it is a question whether any of the applications now in use are of any value in their extermination. None of the old remedies, so far as I know, will do it, and the vaporizing of tobacco is of such recent origin it is impossible to say what its effect on them may be. Fortunately their appearance is at a season of the year when their depredations do not occasion the loss they would at an earlier date.

Mealy Bugs are exceedingly annoying, but it is not often they attack roses if there are other plants at hand more congenial to their taste. Should their presence be detected, look the plants over and remove by hand any nests that may have been formed, as their web is water proof. Those scattered on the plants can be exterminated by a few applications of kerosene emulsion. Different formulas have been given for this by various writers, the best of which I think is the following: Take equal parts of kerosene and fir tree oil; mix this with water in the proportion of 3 per cent. to 97 of of water, and apply through a fine hand syringe in the morning an hour before syringing, at which time wash the foliage well, and no harm will follow. Applied in this manner two or three times in ten days, will rid the plants of them. One grower recommends one part of kerosene to thirty-two of water, the application to be made in the same manner. I have never been able to discover that tobacco had any effect upon them; in fact, they rather seem to like it than otherwise, and in this respect at least, lay claim to what is popularly supposed to be a luxury belonging to a higher order of beings. They especially love coleus, but for use on this plant the proportion of kerosene given should be lessened one third, or injury may result.

Although at times the "Thousand Legged Worm" appears in quantity, I know of but little harm arising from them save in their disturbance of the soil. If present on the benches, they will often enter a pot through the drainage, and the presence of several in a small pot will check root action. Both air slacked lime and fine tobacco sprinkled over the bench will kill those it reaches.

I remember once filling a solid bed for roses, in the soil of which the germs must have been present in quantity, as, early in the spring multitudes appeared on the surface. These were most of them killed by covering the surface two inches thick with tobacco stems, leaving them there a week before being removed.

Experiments were also made at that time with a solution of potash in water, with good results.

Perhaps one of the most destructive enemies of the rose is the White Grub. We occasionally hear of whole benches being destroyed by these pests, often after the plants are one-third grown. If suitable care is taken in the preparation of the soil this should not occur. A season rarely passes in which some are not found, and it is well to have a few plants grown in pots to a good size, with which to replace such as may be destroyed. Keep these shifted and in good growing condition so that as little time may be lost as possible if it is necessary to use them. If some morning you notice a plant wilting while all around it are doing well, you may be pretty sure the roots have been severed by this grub. Remove the plant and search every inch of soil around it until the grub is found, or in a few days another will succumb to its ravages. When present in a bench there is no other way of stopping their work, but the better way is not to let them enter the house. As is well known, they are nearly always present in sod, and sometimes when the supply has run short and I have been obliged to cut some just before planting, it has been thoroughly examined and if any were found every portion of it has been carefully handled and all the grubs destroyed. This is slow work and should be avoided, but it must be done where soil is for any reason provided late in the season, or a whole crop may be ruined. Other means of prevention will be found under the head of "The Preparation of Soil."

It is doubtful if anything in the line of insect enemies has ever caused more anxiety to rose growers, where they have obtained a strong foothold, than has the insect which causes what is known as Club Root. See Fig. 27.

Evidently this is no new disease, it having been observed in various species of plants, and occasionally roses have been subject to it in individual cases. It is the cause that is new, and for its discovery we are indebted, I believe, to Prof. Halstead, of New Jersey, and the illustration of it used here is the same as used by him in his description of it in a recent number of the *American Florist*.

He found the cause to be a worm formed somewhat like an eel, and invisible to the naked eye. The knots, or lobes, on the roots are their house, and here they live and multiply. The writer remembers to have seen what he now believes to have been the same thing, many

Fig. 27.

years ago, and little doubt exists in his mind but that their presence at that time was due to the use of manure which came from the cattle pens of a distillery, although the manure was two years old when applied. Inquiries have been heard for several years from one and another as to what was the cause of the trouble, but not until quite recently has it become so serious as to demand special investigation, some growers having lost whole houses through its ravages within a year or two. When a plant is seriously attacked by club root, the growth ceases, or at least is very feeble; the foliage turns a light yellowish green, similar to a plant when it is said to be "water logged." The edges of the leaves in some cases seem to burn, turn brown and dry up; in fact, the plant looks, as one writer expresses it, "as though it had the grippe." Such a plant, if lifted, will show more or less of these knotty roots. Should a majority of the plants in a bed become infested, it will be better to remove and destroy both them and the soil they were in by fire at once, as there is no known remedy at present which will kill them and at the same time restore life and vigor to the plants. These are supposed to be brought into the houses in the summer, either by being present in the soil or manure, or both, and as it is apparent no remedy will easily be found to cure, it seems to me attention should be turned to preventive measures. Some have advocated heating the soil. This is not practicable, as not only the insect, but the life of the soil would be destroyed, were the temperature raised sufficiently to kill the first. Dr. Halstead tells us frost will kill them. If this is the case, let those who are troubled with them to an extent endangering their crop, try this method of prevention. To do it effectually, prepare the soil pile in the usual way, but do it in the summer, and early enough to admit of turning once or twice. With the appearance of winter, spread out the pile thin enough to have it freeze solid. After this has taken place, the soil can again be gathered in a pile. Should a trial prove this to be a sure preventive, it would pay to erect an open shed under which to spread and freeze the soil, and thus prevent it from being leached by the fall and winter rains. If there is any suspicion of their presence in the manure, the same method should be used with that also. This is, of course, practicable only in latitudes where freezing weather prevails. The writer already quoted gives it as his opinion that the greater prevalence of this trouble the past two years, is to be attributed to the fact that, during that time, the winters have been unusually mild in sections where the most complaint is heard. Were I troubled with this pest I should certainly give this method of prevention a thorough trial, and I trust those who are will do so the coming season, if they are located in sections where the elements will come to their aid. This I know will entail quite an additional amount of work, but it seems to be a case similar to that of a man with a gangrenous limb,—the choice is to part with either limb or life. So in this, as it seems to me, the most serious matter connected with rose growing that has ever come to our knowledge, the cause must be overcome, or the business abandoned where they have taken possession.

Another precautionary measure is, never to propagate from any plants which have become infested with this disease, even in the least.

It is my belief that wherever these nematoids are present in the roots, even if only one cell has been formed, their power to multiply and spread to other roots on the same plant must be accomplished through the circulation of the sap of the plant. So very minute are their eggs they may be conveyed to any part of the plant through this circulating medium. Sever a cutting containing any of these eggs, root it, and what assurance is there that it will not be the home of a future colony. Some investigations right along this line, made by one interested in them, were recently witnessed by the writer. The rooted cutting of a rose was the subject. This was rooted in clean sand which had been taken from a bank fifteen feet below the surface. The callus was reduced to pulp, put under a powerful microscope, and in it could be seen distinctly two living nematoids. Under a lens of 300 diameters, these appeared to be about $\frac{1}{16}$ of an inch in length. Where did they come from, unless the germs were present in the sap, and descended to the callus as that grew, where they developed into the forms revealed by the microscope? Evidently there is still opportunity, as well as a great call, for the further study of this much to be dreaded pest.

Green fly is the name by which the most common of all insects is famililarly known, but Prof. Baker denominates it " The Rose Plant Louse." Its method of attack is like that of the spider, puncturing the plant and absorbing its juices. Although not as dangerous an enemy of the rose as many already described, because it can more easily be kept at bay, still from September to May it will be found ever present if measures are not taken to prevent it. Its power of reproduction almost passes belief.

Prof. Baker tells us, " one single louse might have in one summer six thousand million descendants." The danger to be apprehended from them is from neglect. If this occurs for a short time, even a few days, some of them will have attained a size and strength which makes it difficult to kill them, while in number, the smaller ones will be legion.

There is no excuse whatever for the person who allows them to attain any size, or even to be seen. It is simple neglect on the part of the one in charge, where this state of things exists, as there are many devices for their prevention.

CHAPTER XXVII.

INSECT EXTERMINATORS.

Tobacco smoke has been the most common agent used in the destruction of insect life, but to fumigate houses of cut flowers so injures some varieties, other means of applying it have been sought that would accomplish the same result without damage to delicate blooms.

Scattering dry stems through the walks or under the benches will do it, but to this there are two objections. The untidy appearance the houses present, and the cost, if stems have to be purchased, for to do it effectually in this way, requires large quantities. Others advocate the use of tobacco dust sprinkled on the foliage, but for roses this is impracticable on account of the frequent syringing required.

Some who heat by steam have tried evaporating liquid tobacco in galvanized iron troughs, and strongly recommend this method. Not heating with steam myself, I have not tried and cannot speak of it from experience. I have tried the same plan on hot water pipes, but found they were not hot enough to evaporate the liquid. When steam is used, this objection does not prevail, but in the early fall and late spring, those who have used it, tell me other means must be adopted, as it raises the temperature of the houses too high, unless special pipes are arranged for this purpose and radiation from them prevented. At all seasons of the year, when this objection does not exist, it is doubtless the most simple way, and one making the least trouble. For a house 100x18, four troughs are recommended.

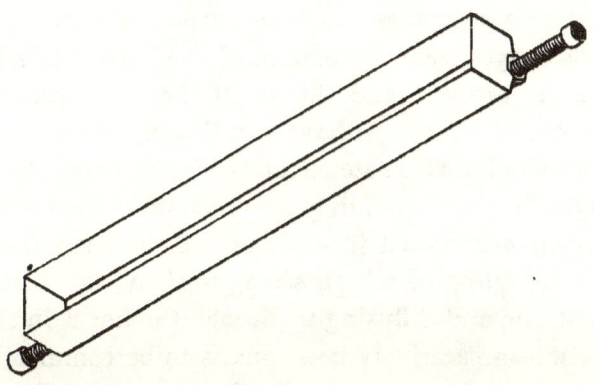

Fig. 27.

In order not to have any liquid remain unevaporated, they may be constructed as shown in fig. 27. A size three feet long by four inches deep and wide, will be sufficient. To prevent them from leaking where the pipe passes through the ends, make a running thread on each piece thus running through, say six inches long, and this will admit of using a rubber packing, and a nut on each side of the galvanized iron, rendering it perfectly tight, and capable of resisting any expansion or contraction there may be in the pipe. If the extract of tobacco is evaporated in these twice a week, scarcely a fly will be seen, provided they are not allowed to multiply and become mature before it is applied. Another plan that is being used in some establishments is, to have two or more half barrels filled with dry stems and placed in the south walk about thirty feet apart. A steam jet is then conveyed to each through pipes arranged for the purpose, the steam being discharged near the bottom of the barrel; this liberates the nicotine and the air of the house becomes impregnated with it. I have seen this in operation and think well of it where stems can be obtained cheaply, although the labor attending it is much more than where extract is evaporated in a somewhat similar manner.

The mingling of a high strength of tobacco extract with steam, and diffusing it through the house in that form, is comparatively new, but is to be commended for the following reasons: Its cleanliness; no dust or litter attend its distribution; no odor remains to offend those to whom it is disagreeable; the rapidity with which it can be administered, saving much valuable time; its reasonable cost.

Observations made last season were so favorable, I went to the expense of a complete outfit in September, and am now using it with great satisfaction. Finding it necessary to change the boiler that tempered the water used, one was set that can be changed at will from that purpose to that of raising the amount of steam necessary for vaporizing the tobacco. To all those who are heating by steam, no change will be necessary, save to supply the pipe and fixtures needed, and I think on all large places heated by water the time is not far distant

INSECT EXTERMINATORS.

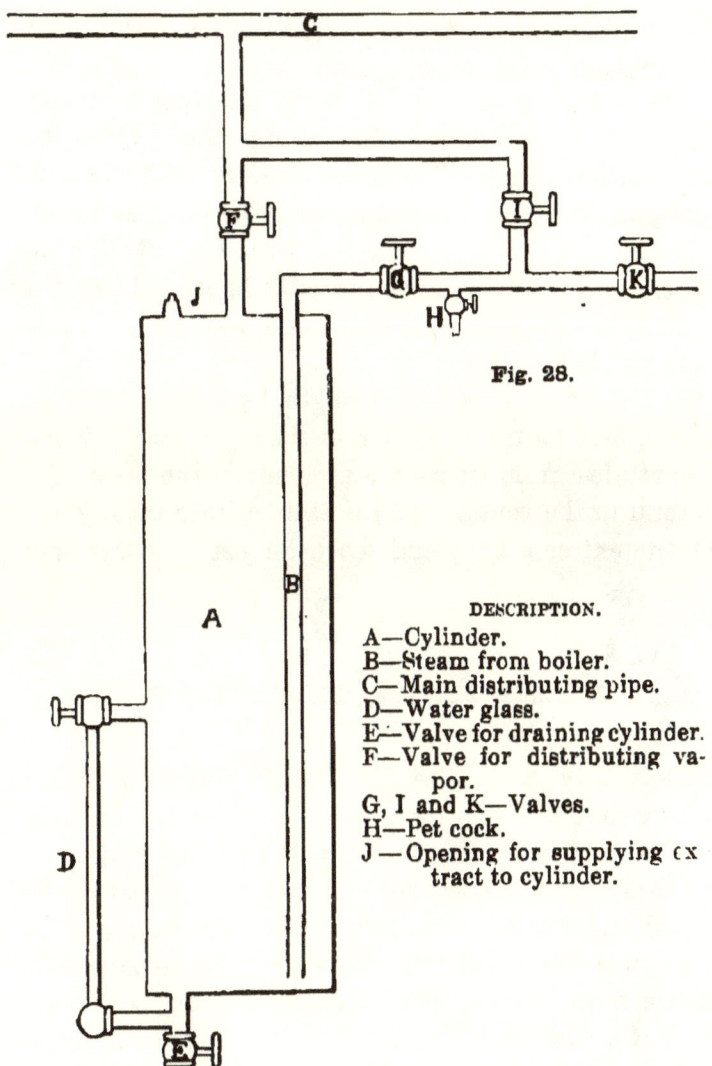

Fig. 28.

DESCRIPTION.

A—Cylinder.
B—Steam from boiler.
C—Main distributing pipe.
D—Water glass.
E—Valve for draining cylinder.
F—Valve for distributing vapor.
G, I and K—Valves.
H—Pet cock.
J—Opening for supplying extract to cylinder.

when it will be found to be best to add a power boiler for this and other purposes.

The illustration (Fig. 28) shows all pipes necessary saving those leading into the house through which the vapor is discharged. These may be of three-fourths inch gas pipe, and after connecting with the main and placing a cut off valve at some convenient point, drop to where they are to be carried into the house. The point where it enters should be under and near the south side of a middle bench.

If the house is 100 feet in length, have three openings in the pipe for the liberation of the vapor; the first one twenty feet from where the pipe enters the house, the second in the centre, and the third within twenty feet of the extreme end, and when in use this last may

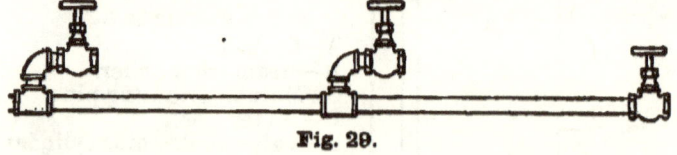

Fig. 29.

be left fully open. See Fig. 29. The opening in the centre should be half-inch, while that nearest the main feed should not be over three-eighths. These variations in the size of the discharge will materially assist in the equalization of the distribution, and if so arranged as to discharge in a straight line with the pipe, no harm will ensue from burning or scalding either root or foliage.

If it is desired to use this line of pipe for any other

purpose, such as the burning of sulphur in early fall, it will be necessary to equip each discharge with valves, and, although this adds to the expense, it will, I think, be found to be the best way. One of the objects I had in view when thinking of adopting this system, was the suppression of mildew in the early fall by use of the same set of pipes.

In laying these pipes, raise the main distributing one to the height wanted; then, from that point to the extreme end of the discharge pipe, let the fall be gradual, in order that no condensation may ever remain in them.

All the mains through which the vapor passes, should be well protected with asbestos, or some other covering, as it is very important in the line of economy, that no condensation occurs while the vapor is being used.

It is best to so arrange the pipes as to be able to vaporize the houses in blocks of four or eight. For the former number, the main from the cylinder, as well as the feed from the boiler, should be of one and a quarter inch pipe, all the other connections about the cylinder may be of inch if preferred. If it is desired to vaporize eight at once, one and three-fourths inch mains should be used.

Of strong manufactured extract, one half pint is allowed to a house of 100 feet. If four houses are to be vaporized, place one quart of extract in cylinder A by means of a funnel at J, after which replace the plug or whatever is used for closing the aperture. If it is desired, a supply tank can be connected with the cylinder at J and operated by a valve, but the first method is preferable and is little trouble, and one then knows just the amount used. With all valves closed except the four three-quarter ones leading direct from the main to the different houses, as well as those through which the vapor passes into the houses from the same sized pipe, open the one at K, examining by pet cock H if there is any condensation in the feed pipe. If not, close pet cock and open valve G, which will admit steam to the cylinder A, which it will fill and soon be ready for distribution. To avoid the condensation of the vapor, it is necessary that all pipes used for its distribution should be hot when it is admitted to them. By closing now for a short time valve G and opening valve I, direct steam from the boiler will accomplish this, and as soon as steam is discharged from the extreme end of the distributing pipes, close valve I, open valve G, also in a moment after, valve F, and the vapor will at once be distributed through the houses. From three to five minutes will be required to empty the cylinder of nicotine.

Steam then being shut out of the cylinder by closing valve G, all pressure will soon pass off into the main through valve F. When this is accomplished, another quart may be supplied through point J, and the same process repeated for the next four houses, taking care to close the valves to those already finished, and opening those that are to receive the next treatment.

If eight houses are to be vaporized at once, instead of four, the process is the same except that double the amount of extract must be supplied to the cylinder.

With the price of extract at $1.50 per gallon, the cost of material will be about 10 cents per house.

To avoid condensation and make quick work, about fifty pounds steam pressure should be indicated and maintained until through, and whatever is used for a cylinder it should be strong enough to stand that amount of pressure. I am using, at present, a common range boiler, three and one-half feet in length by one in diameter, but before being set up it should be tested by means of either steam or hydraulic pressure.

The thing to be most guarded against, is the condensation of the steam and consequent weakening of the extract, as well as the condensation of the vapor itself while being applied. If the latter occurs, the extract will drip from the end of the distributing pipe, while it should all be sent into the house mingled with the steam. No water should ever be allowed to enter the cylinder with the extract, and when through, valve E should be opened and any sediment remaining washed out, otherwise stoppage, may occur in either the feeds to the glass or the pet cock H.

Another thing to be avoided is entrance to a house while the process is going on, or for a short time after the vapor has been applied, as the nicotine sometimes affects either the eyes or stomach unpleasantly. The writer had occasion to nurse a pair of sore eyes for two weeks after his first experiment, the temptation being very great at that time to see if it was strong enough to accomplish what was intended. It should be applied at a time when all ventilation can be dispensed with. If a night fireman is employed, and it will not interfere with the usual circulation, it is well to do it early in the morning, an hour or more before working hours commence. It can also be done in the evening, and the moisture seen upon the leaves after its use very soon disappears and no harm seems to arise from it. I consider the morning hour, however, far preferable during the winter months, while in the fall and early spring it will be found more convenient to attend to it after work has ceased, and the sun disappeared.

Two applications a week, and no fly need ever be seen, nor have any who have used it ever noticed any injurious effects either on foliage or flower, so far as I am able to learn. If applied only once a week, one pint to a house will be found necessary, which will make the cost about twenty cents.

The tobacco extract used is what is known as "Rose Leaf." This is a highly concentrated article, and may also be used where the heating system is hot water, in the following manner :

"Apply the extract pure on the pipes when they are hot, using an ordinary paint brush for the purpose. The heat from the pipes will soon evaporate the moist-

Insect Exterminators 117

ure in the extract, leaving more or less of a dry deposit on the pipes. This should be moistened with water the next day and on the following day renewed with pure extract. Repeat this general programme as necessary, depending of course upon the condition of the houses as to freedom from insects. In exceptional cases it may be necessary to put the pure extract on the pipes every day for two or three days, but the exact line of procedure in these cases of exception can, of course, only be determined by the personal judgment of the party in charge of the house."

There is still another method very convenient on a small place, and exceedingly handy when it is desired to treat only a few houses. Its work is thorough when used for green fly, but has no perceptible effect on young scale, spider or mealy bug, as claimed by some for vaporized extract. It also possesses the merit of great simplicity. Procure three oil stoves having a four-inch burner. Place one in the south walk of a hundred foot house, and the others within twenty feet of either end. Take two and one-half pounds of prepared tobacco dust and divide into three parts. A very convenient dish for holding this is a common tin pie plate. Give each its proportion, place the plates on top of the stoves and turn up the flame, but not enough to have it smoke, and leave until consumed, which should take about half an hour. This process precipitates the killing properties of the tobacco with very little smoke. For a house longer than one hundred feet, more stoves should be used, as, at a cost of seventy-nine cents each, it is not economy to spend time watching and moving one to all parts of the house. The tobacco can be obtained of any one keeping florists' supplies, at a cost of about four cents per pound, and if used twice a week, either at night or on cloudy days, no green fly will be seen.

If one or two tablespoonfuls of tobacco extract are added to the portion of fine tobacco that is directly over the flame of the lamp, it will add to the strength, and the killing properties will be greatly increased. If through neglect the fly has become old and strong, this for a first appplication is very effective, and it will also destroy such "thousand legged" worms as chance to be out of the soil.

This remedy, while simple and effective, cannot be used on such varieties of rose buds as are injured by the use of strong tobacco smoke.

For roses grown in the open air, Ellwanger recommends spraying them with clear water, dusting them afterwards with powdered white hellebore.

CHAPTER XXVIII.
DISEASES OF THE ROSE.

The common saying that "Death loves a shining mark" we find exemplified in vegetable, as well as physical life, and while many strong plants which produce beautiful flowers seem to be in a measure exempt, the Queen of all is very susceptible to many forms, among which the most common is mildew. This is a fungoid growth and is produced by sudden changes in the atmosphere, or drafts of air. As with man or beast, the power of resistance to disease which a plant is able to put forth, is in proportion to its state of health and vigor.

Pampered, sickly plants that have been poorly ventilated or overfed, are fit subjects for any form of disease, and especially liable to this.

The first great preventative is a sturdy, hardy growth. An abundance of air from the time the plant has its first shift, is what makes it sturdy. I do not mean that they should be exposed to drafts of cool air, but that if accustomed to receive all the air possible without this exposure, they will be in condition to withstand the changes that come with the varying seasons.

Some roses are much more susceptible to mildew than others, and unfortunately they are our most valued varieties and cannot be dispensed with. With the advent of early fall the trouble begins, and unless the utmost care is given to methods of ventilation, a little fire started to drive out dampness on a wet day, or temper sudden atmospheric changes, before one is aware of it, the seeds of mildew are sown and the battle with it must commence at once lest it gain a foothold, and if this occurs as late as October and is not conquered immediately, nine times out of ten all profit from that house is gone for the season. Both Mermet and Bride are peculiarly susceptible to this fungus, and no matter how fine the buds may be, if the beauty of the foliage is destroyed by this unsightly discoloration, they are practically valueless for sale as cut flowers.

There is no season of the year in which plants require to be so closely guarded against mildew as during the months of September and October. After the weather becomes cool enough for fires to be regularly maintained, it is much easier to prevent its appearance. The methods of prevention or cure vary with different growers, but the basis of nearly all remedies is sulphur in some form. An occasional painting of the flow pipe after fires are started, with a wash made of sulphur and water with enough water slacked lime to hold it together—say one-tenth—will keep it in check. Another method is to thicken linseed oil with sulphur, and apply in the same way. To either prevent or conquer before this time, the same method may be employed through the medium of the pipe used for vaporizing. Extend this pipe temporarily nearly to the end of the house, put on an ell, raise from it another piece to such a point

DISEASES OF THE ROSE.

as it is convenient to carry through the end of the house. Cap this end with a pet cock or valve, leaving the same partially open for the discharge of condensation. This pipe may be painted as already described with the sulphur wash, or two small galvanized iron troughs as seen on page 109 can be permanently placed on this pipe, a small quantity of the wash evaporated from them, while the balance of the pipe is wrapped to prevent radiation of heat when not wanted in the house. In this way, all houses needing it can be served at once by turning the steam into the vaporizing main. Two applications a week will in most cases prevent its gaining a foothold. Various formulas are also recommended by those who have used them. After preparing them they are applied to the foliage in the form of a spray. The oldest of these is the one given by Peter Henderson many years since.

"Boil 3 pounds of sulphur and 3 pounds of lime in 6 gallons of water until it is reduced to 2 gallons; allow the liquid to settle until it becomes clear, then put it in a jar, or bottle it for use. Use one gill of this to 5 gallons of water and apply to the foliage by means of a syringe."

To this there are two objections. It can not be procured ready for use, and appliances for compounding it are not always at hand. Another objection is, no matter how carefully the liquid is poured off after boiling, the lime in it will whiten and thus greatly disfigure the foliage, making the buds unsalable.

Mr. Richard Bagg gives the following, which is more easily prepared and leaves no discoloration:

"Put a three inch pot full of flour of sulphur into an earthen vessel, to which add water sufficient to form it into a paste, being careful to have all the sulphur wet. To this add an equal amount of broken caustic potash, stir again and it will rapidly assume an orange brown color, become very hot and turn liquid. Add now water enough to make a quart, bottle, and it is ready for use. A desert spoonful to a gallon of water used in the form of a spray every day will soon cure; but, as a preventive, use once, twice or three times a week, according to the weather."

Mr. H. M. Wheeler recommends the following:

"Take one pound of sulphur, one of slacked lime, three-fourths of an ounce of carbolic acid, add two gallons of water and boil to one gallon. Cork well and set away for use. Use a two and a half inch pot full to five gallons of water. Keep the ventilators down two or three hours after application to retain the fumes. We use this twice a week, not only as a cure, but a preventive."

The objection to this, if there is any, is in the line of that of Henderson's.

Prof. Maynard of Massachusetts says:

"In the fall of the year I find the use of a small kerosene stove the most convenient form in which to apply sulphur; the same being put in a kettle and boiled

Diseases of the Rose. 123

for a few hours twice a week. The only precaution is to use no more heat than is sufficient to boil the sulphur, for should it catch fire it would damage the plants."

Mr. Sewall Fischer recommends the use of hyposulphite of soda, in the proportion of half an ounce to a gallon of water.

Still another formula, from Mr. R. S. Halliday, is as follows:

"I would recommend the use of sulphuret of potassium in place of flour of sulphur, in the proportion of two ounces to twenty-four gallons of water. Syringe with the mixture once in two weeks, or oftener if you see any signs of the fungus appearing. I have also found it a remedy for black spot."

Dry sulphur applied directly to the foliage by means of a bellows or by beating it from a cheese cloth bag, is also used by many, and after applying, the house is kept closed for an hour and the temperature allowed to rise to about 100°.

One objection to the various washes lies in the fact that if used too strong, they will cause the foliage to drop, while in plants badly affected, the wash needs to be used thoroughly, and this necessitates incurring some risk. If sulphur is used in the dry state and care is not taken to distribute evenly and in small quantity, the result sought will not be accomplished, more will be required, which the subsequent syringing will carry to the soil.

I do not remember to have seen harm from this, but it should be avoided as much as possible on general principles, for certainly no one would recommend the use of sulphur in the soil.

I have known of several, belonging to the class of those who think "if little is good, more is better," who have tried burning the pure article on a hot brick, or by throwing some among the tobacco while fumigating, thinking thus to relieve the plants of the fungus. They succeeded, and were able to carry out both fungus and leaves at the same time. This cannot occur when applied to the flow pipes as a wash, and the fumes produced in this way accomplish the purpose at a minimum of risk.

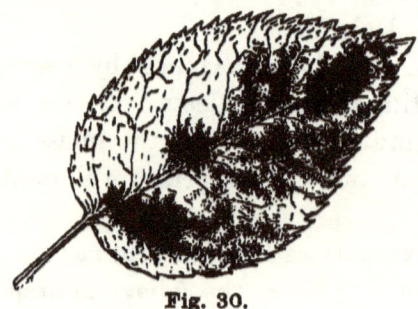

Fig. 30.

Black spot is another fungoid disease. Prof. Windle, of Purdue University, illustrated an article upon this subject, with views of the disease obtained through the use of the microscope, and I am indebted to him for the illustrations used here. This fungus appears to the naked eye like black spots on the surface of the leaves as seen in fig. 30. The growth is rapid and soon assumes form under the glass as seen in fig. 31. Prof. Seymour tells us these throw off spores which float in the air and impregnate healthy tissues. See Fig. 32.

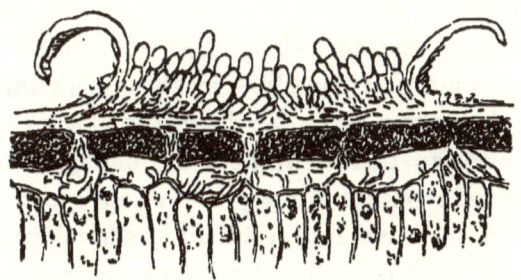

Fig. 31.

The reason why some varieties are more liable to its ravages than others, is not easy of explanation. That it is oftener present in teas containing an admixture of hybrid blood is unquestioned, and would seem to confirm the theory of some that it is engendered by such crosses. I am more inclined to think it is transmitted, and that for some reason unknown to us, the cross

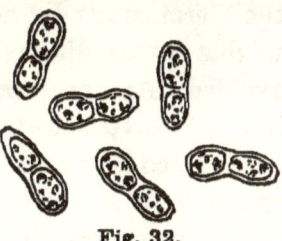

Fig. 32.

is much more subject to it than is the parent hybrid. It is rarely seen in a true tea-rose unless it has been subjected to contagious influences, while many of the hybrids cannot be grown in the open air on account of its ravages.

Of the many hybrid teas which have appeared within the last ten years and have been given a trial, none remain in general use save La France, and both this and American Beauty need careful handling in order to keep the disease at bay.

It will have been noticed by those who grow hybrids in the open air, that usually they show comparatively little tendency to take on the disease until late summer or early autumn, then with the heavy dews, cool nights and scorching sun at midday it develops rapidly, ofttimes stripping the plants of foliage in a few days. The same conditions, though in less severe form, will have the same effect on both La France and Beauty under glass. I have seen a house of the former ruined in three days, by an over watered bench being exposed for a short time to a sudden change of temperature, though the thermometer did not fall below fifty. This teaches us that the conditions producing this result must be avoided. Another means of prevention is perfect cleanliness. Leaves showing the disease should be removed and burned as fast as they appear, thus preventing the spores from maturing and spreading. Having been careful to observe the preventives mentioned, I have not had a serious case of spot for some years, consequently have had no occasion to prove the remedies others have advocated, but enumerate them here for the benefit of any who desire to give them a trial.

Jean Sisley recommends spraying the foliage with a solution of salt water, in the proportion of six pounds of salt to twenty-four gallons of water.

Mr. Halliday finds the remedy he gives for mildew, as found on page 123, beneficial for this also, while both Mr. Wheeler and Mr. Fisher recommend their compound for this form of fungus.

In relation to its cure Prof. Halstead says: "This trouble may be held in check by the carbonate of copper compound, using three ounces of carbonate of copper, one quart of ammonia and fifty gallons of water. The spraying should be done once a week, using a hose and nozzle that gives a fine spray. The point should be to wet every part of the plant and yet not to drench it."

After giving the whole matter careful study, I have come to the conclusion that wherever it is met with in an advanced stage, it is more the fault of the grower than the plant—that is, the laws governing a healthy plant growth have not been observed, thus inviting this disease to fasten upon an impaired vitality, no matter which of the various causes producing that state of things has been the medium through which the disease has been invited.

CHAPTER XXIX.

FORCING VARIETIES—CULTURAL NOTES.

The number of forcing varieties suitable for continuous winter flowering, is exceedingly limited. Many varieties which are simply grand under glass in summer, are utterly worthless for winter work, and the reverse is also true of some of our best winter bloomers. Perle des Jardins undoubtedly stands at the head of the list as an all the year around rose, and still, if not properly treated, or if the weather is for a long time unfavorable during the winter months, its buds will be more or less imperfect. The conditions being favorable, and particularly the nights being cool, the most perfect specimens are produced in the month of October, and again in March on plants that were set late, and have bloomed lightly previous to that date, and this will occur without any specially prepared soil. To insure paying results during November, December and January, while the days are shortest and often sunless, is a conundrum that has confronted many a grower. I am satisfied so-called "bullheads" may be attributed largely to four causes: Too heavy soil, excessive feed, a low temperature, absence of sun heat.

All these influences have a direct bearing, and singly or combined, each plays a part in producing unsatisfactory results.

It can be accepted as a fixed rule, that all varieties which do well in summer heat, need a higher temperature in winter than the average standard. Applying this to Perle, we find it does not require as high a degree of heat in summer to bring it to perfection, as do Mad. Margottin, Etoile de Lyon and others that might be mentioned. From this we reason that the degree of temperature given it should be above the average, but still under the maximum. Repeated trials have convinced me that in my soil the night temperature best suited to Perle during the three dark months, is 62°, and prefer 63° to 60° or 61°. Allusion has previously been made to a trial of this rose in a heavy soil, and the unfavorable result that followed. If your soil is very heavy and you have not the means of lightening it, the temperature will need to be some higher, 63° to 65°. A light loam is undoubtedly the best, and if that is not at hand, reduce the texture of your soil by the addition of one-fourth clean sand. Let the compost used be old and well decomposed. Mix all thoroughly by turning several times before bringing into the house. I would not advise the use of bone meal for this variety except in a very small quantity, until January, being careful during December not to mulch or feed heavily. From the time the buds are wanted until October, the quality of the buds will be greatly enhanced by disbudding all laterals, but after this date this should not be practiced, as throwing all the sap to the centre bud tends to malform it. On the contrary, from this time until spring, the buds should be watched as they form, and if the centre one on the strong shoots shows any tendency to curve or cling its petals, it should be removed at once, thus giving the strength of the plant to the development of laterals, which will usually form fine buds. With the turn of the season and strong sunlight, liberal treatment may be used with safety and disbudding resumed. As this is really the only yellow rose that can be relied upon for winter work at present, a vacancy occurs and a want is felt if it is not in good form.

A careful observance of the foregoing suggestions, together with an intelligent application of general cultural treatment, and I do not think any grower will have cause to complain that this rose does not pay him.

Meteor is one of the roses requiring a high summer temperature to develop it perfectly, and possesses some characteristics which render it almost indispensable. It is the only rose of its color available during the winter months. Its habit of throwing single terminal buds instead of clusters is in its favor, while the length of stem and foliage that can be given with each bud materially increases its value for retailing. It revels in a temperature of sixty-eight to seventy and will need more heat by day than others. Still, air must be given, and in sufficient quantity to keep the house pure and sweet. It is very sensitive to sudden changes and takes on mildew easily, hence careful watch is necessary. During the short days, should any of the canes throw buds in cluster form, remove the center one as soon as it forms. Spider, also, quickly gains a foothold with this variety, not that it is a favorite, and toothsome above all others, but on account of the higher temperature, coupled with the tendency the larger leaves have to cup slightly, making it necessary to be careful about syringing, and to see that all under surfaces are reached. It is a rose that cannot be spared, and should be found in every collection where enough are grown to be able to give it a house by itself, or in connection with another requiring the same amount of heat, and even where this cannot be done, those growing for their own retail trade, will find it to add greatly to their assortment if given a warm corner in one of their houses.

Catherine Mermet, all things considered, has been, up to the present time, the leading favorite in pink. Its habit of bleaching in dark weather is against it, but when in perfect form and color, nothing of this shade, in the opinion of many, approaches it in beauty.

Unlike the preceding rose, this requires a temperature below the average, and is practically worthless six months in the year, because it cannot be grown cool enough. For this reason diligence should be exercised to have it in good producing form by the last of October, and this necessitates early planting, as well as constant care. It is not reasonable to expect a large cut of buds during the winter, unless there is a correspondingly large and strong plant from which to grow them. Spring work and sales often reach into the summer months, retarding both shifting and planting. The loss resulting, is noticeable in this variety more than in some others, owing to the limited time during which the buds mature perfectly; hence it is of the utmost importance they should be planted early, in order that they may have a large amount of bud producing wood by the last week in October.

As previously stated, the soil best adapted to the growth of Mermet is a stiff loam with little if any admixture of sand. They are strong feeders, and will repay anything administered to them intelligently. When a new growth is forming, and just before the buds set, the tendency to go blind can be controlled to a certain extent, by applying a little less water to the roots for a few days, but syringe the foliage as usual. Neither should stimulants of any kind be given in this stage—either apply when the breaks are commencing, or else after the buds are set. Quality is always produced at the expense of quantity, and if large, perfect buds are desired, the night temperature should not be above fifty-five, and if it occasionally falls to fifty or fifty-two, no harm will result, providing the plants are hardy and if sufficient air is given to keep the day temperature well in hand.

This rose is more liable to mildew than some of the other teas, and requires constant watchfulness. I have seen the entire crop for the two best paying months in the year, utterly ruined by one day's carelessness. Some one has said, "Success in this business depends upon constant watchfulness every moment, every hour, twenty-four hours each day and three hundred and sixty-five days in the year," and if true of any variety, it is doubly so of this.

For a fancy white, nothing as yet equals the Bride—Victoria being of too recent introduction to have been able to prove her claim to first place. As the Bride is a sport from Mermet, partaking of all the characteristics of that plant, save in color, conditions suitable to the development of the latter are applicable to this also.

We have another useful white in Niphetos, and this is the most prolific rose in cultivation, as well as the purest white. It is not a strong grower, and if used on its own roots should be planted on a south bench near the glass. Purchasers sometimes find fault because this is not as large as stronger growing varieties bought at the same price. This cannot be expected unless the plants have had one or two more months in which to grow than their more vigorous companions. For this reason this is another variety requiring time in which to make flowering wood, and should be made from strong cuttings, as early in the year as the wood is in prime condition. If they attain good size in the bench, it will not pay to flower them the second season. If planted late and they have not grown too large, they may, perhaps, do good work the second year, if one cannot obtain new and better stock. The only way promising success, if they are to be carried over, is to withhold water from them in May until the wood is ripened, prune them back, take up, shake out all the soil, and pot in as small pots as will well contain the roots. Set in a shaded place outside, and as soon as they have formed roots that will hold the ball together give one shift, move to a sunny place, and when well established plant where they are to remain for the winter. Far finer buds can be obtained by budding as described on page 61, (Roses for Summer), the ground where the stocks are to remain having been excavated to a good depth. drainage supplied, and a quantity of rich soil filled in. Niphetos will thrive in a moderately high or low temperature. If quantity is desired, keep them at sixty-three to five. If quality, on budded stock, fifty-five to fifty-eight. At fifty the flowers will be of monstrous size, but correspondingly less in quantity. The petals of this rose being so delicate in both structure and color, excessive dampness, as well as tobacco smoke even in moderate quantity, is equally disastrous.

For a lighter color in red than Meteor, Papa Gontier supplies the place so long held by the now nearly obsolete Bon Silene, of which it is a seedling. This rose seems to do well in any good rose soil, if porous and well drained. It matures best in a cool atmosphere, not over fifty-six at night, and with an abundance of air by day, but is impatient of sudden changes or too wet soil. While the wood is of good size, it does not grow as rapidly as some varieties; root action is not so vigorous; for these reasons it will not absorb so much water, and requires a fleet bench, not over four inches of soil, and this well drained. If you discover in it a tendency to shed its leaves, look for sudden changes in temperature or over watering as the cause. To show at their best, the buds should be cut before they are open at the tip, and be placed in water under the cellar skylight until matured. One who has not tried this will be astonished at the transformation that will take place in a few days. Sometimes in cold weather four days after cutting will be required to develop them perfectly and show them at their best. If exposed to the light and no ice allowed to come near them in the cellar they will retain their fine coloring and be of twice the value they were when first cut.

All lovers of color admire the silvery pink of La France, and in popular favor it stands second only to Mermet, while with many it occupies first place. It is by no means a difficult rose to grow, though somewhat delicate in comparison with others. It loves a soil suitable for Perle, but as it is subject to black spot, watering and atmospheric changes must be carefully attended to. To develop well it should be grown in a temperature varying but little from sixty-two at night.

The buds should never be cut until well expanded, which detracts from its value as a shipping rose. Within a few hours from the time they are open, they should be on the market, undergoing in the meantime as little handling as possible, the delicacy of both petals and color—which makes them such favorites—forbidding what to some varieties is a benefit.

White La France, a rose of exceedingly delicate coloring, and a favorite in some sections, requires much the same treatment as that already described for La France.

American Beauty supplies both form and color not found in any of the foregoing. Not all who try, succeed with it, but the cause of failure is not always easy to determine. Some who succeed once, fail on the next trial, and it is desirable that all the conditions of both success and failure should be made a subject of careful study. No one would dare lay down any set formula of treatment, as may be done with some varieties, for all such are liable to fail, as the writer has had the opportunity of proving.

This dear rose—in more senses than one—is exceedingly capricious, and often found in the condition in which a cynic once classed her glorious namesake, "when she will she will, and when she wont she wont." I venture the assertion, however, that he whose perceptions are keen enough to match the latter, will usually succeed with the first also. Were I to venture any cultural suggestions they would be the following:

Give it the same soil as Mermet, plant early, the last of May if possible, and with good strong plants that have never been allowed to become pot bound. Do not let the night temperature fall below 58° or exceed 63°. Should very thick, heavy canes come up from the bottom, that will not form a bud when left to mature, pinch off such as they appear when from twelve to fifteen inches high, and from one to four side shoots will form that are pretty sure to bud. Strong shoots that go blind will, if bent over, usually throw blooming shoots from the lower buds, or from the base of the plant. It is a ravenous feeder and you must do well by it if you would see a fine growth.

The remaining roses used for winter work are mainly duplicates in color of those already described. Among these, Sunset, a sport from Perle, and Duchess of Albany, from La France, should be given in the main the same treatment as described for the varieties from which they originated. Sunset is less apt to come deformed in winter than its parent, Perle, the buds being formed mainly on single stems instead of in cluster form, as is sometimes the case with the latter. Waban, a sport from Mermet, has, so far as I know, been utterly unable to redeem herself in the estimation of growers, and must be set down as worthless in most localities, but the color so much sought after, as well as good habit, seems to have been found in her sister, the Bridesmaid.

This is also a sister of the Bride and bids fair to rank with her in popular favor. It shows no inclination to throw malformed buds, and holds its color well during long continued dark weather, the only defect which can be found with its illustrious parent. I have had the opportunity of watching this rose for a year, and find treatment accorded Mermet, suited to this also.

Madam Pierre Guillott is another rose not as well

known as some but one highly prized by those who love variegation in color. The ground work of lemon white, daintily bordered with pink, gives us a shade not found in any save Watteville, and superior to that variety in both coloring, productivness and ease with which it is grown. Like many others it is better suited for summer flowering, being seen at its best in early fall and spring. To be made profitable in winter, it should be given a shallow bench near the glass, and grown in a night temperature of from 65° to 68°. It is one of the best keepers we have and exceedingly productive. Those desiring to grow Meteor, and not wishing to plant an entire house of it, will find this to do well in the same temperature, the three south rows of a middle bench, as well as the south bench itself, being well adapted to its growth. Pierre Guillott is another of this class though different in color. It may not require quite so high a temperature as the former, but should not be grown at less than 63°. This also is a better summer than winter rose.

Madam Watteville succeeds well with only a few growers; with me it does best in a soil and temperature suited to La France, but burns easily and needs careful watching and the glass clouded slightly, as soon as the sun commences to take strong effect. It should be allowed to expand well on the bush before cutting, placed in water and kept twenty-four hours before being offered for sale.

Wm. Francis Bennett has been grown less with each passing year, for the reason that it is not an easy rose to cultivate, and that others of nearly the same shade, with which success is more assured, have in a great measure taken its place. Its delicious fragrance, warm color, perfect form and beautiful foliage, made all acquainted with it reluctant to part company with so agreeable a variety, but one by one the growers have abandoned its cultivation. It should be grown at about 60°, allowed to expand fully, cut and placed in a cool cellar for a few hours, when it will gather its petals like a tulip and be ready for a quick sale.

Many who are unable to grow American Beauty to profit, find a substitute for it in some respects in Souv. de Wootton. It will bear very high feed, and if the manure is two years old and well composted, use half manure and half soil. Let the soil used be a stiff strong loam. Grow in a night temperature of from 50° to 55°, and do not allow more than one bud to mature on a cane. If we could all grow such blooms of this as were shown at Toronto in the winter of '90, I very much fear American Beauty would fall into "innocuous desuetude."

If those who cannot grow Beauty successfully, and still desire a rose of that form and color for their own retail trade, will give this a trial under the above conditions, they will find in it a very fair substitute for Beauty save in fragrance.

Mad. Cusin is a rose which seems to succeed wit[h]
only a few, and these few eastern growers. I am fre[e]
to say I have not as yet found what it requires, nor d[o]
I know a western grower who succeeds with it as we[ll]
as they do around New York. Those who have ha[d]
the best success, grow it in a heavy soil and in a nigh[t]
temperature of 58 to 60°. At first sight, it display[s]
but few qualities except prolificness that are calculate[d]
to attract the grower, and the purchaser must also [be]
educated to its use. Unattractive in color by sunligh[t]
its beauty of color is brought out only under gasligh[t.]
Seen thus in masses with an abundance of foliage,
at once chains the attention of all beholders. Th[is]
makes it one of the most popular roses for evenin[g]
decoration.

For a rose to "fill in," used either for cut sprays [or]
as a substitute for white in designs when that col[or]
cannot be obtained, probably no one rose grown t[o-]
day answers the purpose better than Clothilde Soupe[rt.]
Though worthless from a commercial standpoint, it [is]
valuable to the small grower for home trade, as it w[ill]
grow in almost any good soil, and in a mixed collectio[n.]

The last rose among the older teas worthy of me[n-]
tion in this connection, is Mad. Hoste. It requires [a]
stiff soil, strong feed and a temperature of from 58 [to]
60°. It is very productive, many who grow for the[ir]
own use preferring it to any other of its color, becau[se]
they can, if necessary, substitute it for either Perle

Bride. All weak wood, as well as buds, should be removed, as it has the habit of producing more than it can mature into first-class flowers.

Among the new roses of more recent date, Kaiserina Augusta Victoria and Mad. Testout give great promise, and there is no doubt a place for both if they continue as they have commenced. The former resembles Cornelia Cook in form, more than any now grown, but is much more easily handled than that variety was ever capable of being. It is an exceedingly strong grower, and will undoubtedly become popular wherever a rose of that color is needed for vase decoration, as the foliage is fine and abundant. Mad. Testout resembles La France in many respects, but is a stronger grower, and the blooms larger. It is of too recent origin to be able to say just what treatment is best adapted to its need.

CHAPTER XXX.
THE FORCING OF HYBRIDS.

The difficulties attending hybrid forcing are so great, very few, comparatively, attempt it. In order to be profitable, wholesale prices should range from $100 per 100 at Christmas, to $25.00 per 100 two months later, and the markets are few that encourage a grower to incur the necessary risk. Three methods are employed for blooming this class—the solid border, growing in pots, and in shallow benches. The first of these methods was the only way until within a few years, and General Jacquimenot about the only variety, and there are many fine producing beds of this kind in existence yet. Before planting, the ground should be thoroughly and deeply trenched, tile drainage provided where inclined to be wet, rich soil filled in and planted with budded or grafted stock, as these unquestionably give larger blooms. After blooming they will make their growth for the following season's work, and after this time water should be withheld in order to have the wood ripen early, in some cases scarcely any water being used save that applied to the foliage during the period of growth. Plenty of air should be given, but the sash should be so arranged as to exclude all rain. After two or three severe frosts in the fall, to which they should be exposed, prune them back to strong eyes, clean the house of leaves, give a mulch of cow manure two inches deep and wash this into the soil by a good watering. Bend over and tie all canes so as to fill the space evenly, and for the first week carry a low temperature. As the buds swell and breaks commence, the temperature can be gradually raised, but should not be above fifty until the buds commence to set, which will be in from four to six weeks. During this time, or while the buds are forming, water must be used with great care, but syringing on bright days should be well attended to. After the buds are formed, both water and feed may be supplied

THE FORCING OF HYBRIDS.

more liberally, and from this time the temperature gradually raised to fifty-six or eight. From ten to twelve weeks are required from the time the plants are started until the first buds are ready for market. One thing to be avoided in a crop of this kind is to have it mature to any extent during Lent, but as these dates vary, each grower must figure for himself, taking into account the ripeness of the wood as well as the coolness, or otherwise, of the fall. The blooming period can then be advanced by a week, or retarded several at the option of the operator, by either raising or lowering the temperature of the house. Less risk attends this than other methods, and it is well adapted to the want of those who have a retail trade which will warrant them in devoting a small house to this purpose, but of course early bloom cannot be obtained in this way. Growing hybrids on benches for early bloom is a trade in itself, and requires not only experience but great skill and sound judgment. Although I have tried this method to some extent in years past, the markets of the west have not as yet given the encouragement necessary for supplying this class of stock, consequently I have not given the time and study needed to render success assured in this method. For this reason I give here the system recommended by a prominent eastern grower, who has had great success in this special line.

The Hon. Jno. Burton, who has the reputation of being the best grower of hybrids about Philadelphia, thus states his method of growing them on shallow benches:

"Shallow benches are preferred, not because they will produce more flowers, but for the reason the moisture is under such perfect control they can be produced much earlier than in solid beds. No matter what plan s adopted, there is great uncertainty about getting hybrid roses to bloom early. I have often had a partial failure when the treatment has been as nearly as possible the same as that given in other houses in which the best success was obtained. But when you do obtain them in perfect form it will repay you, whether grown for profit, or for your own pleasure or amusement. A few well finished hybrids on stems two feet long, with fine foliage and good substance of petal, will give as much satisfaction generally, as an armful of teas.

"The houses used for this purpose are of the ordinary pattern, three-fourths span, the benches constructed in the usual way, provided with good drainage and filled with soil five inches deep. For two years past I have used no manure in the soil provided for this work, but have mixed with it flour of bone at the rate of two hundred pounds to a house one hundred feet long Were the soil poor I would also add one load of manure to eight of soil.

"For early planting, two methods are adopted for obtaining the plants needed. They are either soft cuttings taken from the crop flowering the last of December, or, as is more generally the case, plants made from cuttings from the last crop of the previous summer's growth. These should be grown in three-inch pots, rested through November and December, washed out and repotted about January first, and in this way they make fine plants for placing in the border in March or April.

"When planting, place the weaker growers on the low benches, and those required for first flowering should be in position by April, as the growth must be made by the last of July and the plants ready for ripening. Some growers prefer plants budded or grafted on manetta, but if I have a good plant from a three-inch pot, as already described, ready to plant April first, I am satisfied.

"From this time until you are ready to ripen the wood every means must be adopted for producing a strong, rapid growth. Give them plenty of water, and all the air needed for a healthy, sturdy growth. When the days are hot and dry, do not fail to syringe often, in order to keep down red spider, for if there is much of this when it becomes necessary to ripen the wood, as soon as water is withheld the leaves will begin to fall and the result will be, the plant will have neither leaves nor flowers.

"The ripening of the wood is the most important, as well as difficult part of the process. What is sought to be accomplished is to stop the growth, harden the wood and drop the leaves *without loosing the roots*, and this can only be done by the very careful use of water. If they have been getting water every day, use it only every other day, then every third day, but watch carefully that the wood does not shrivel, or the leaves burn. When water is given, do not be afraid of supplying it liberally, for if the plants are kept fresh by syringing, or damping the top soil only, the surface roots will be kept alive, while all below will be dead.

"Two months will be required in which to thoroughly harden the wood. After this is accomplished, prune out all soft and weak wood, leaving from two to four canes, according to the strength of the plant, the chances being that the strongest of these will break from two eyes, and mature buds from each. These canes should be cut back to within from six to twelve inches of the bed, according to the strength of the plant. The house should be cleaned of dead leaves, trimmings and accumulations of any kind, by a thorough sweeping, after which give two or three light waterings to soften the soil. When this has been done, give a top dressing of two inches of strong, fresh cow manure, and water until the bed is well soaked.

"If this is the first house to be brought to bloom, it will now be the last of September or the first of October, so give all the ventilation possible as they will soon start into growth. Syringe every fine day, but be careful about water, as the heavy top dressing will keep them from drying out very fast, and root action has only just commenced. Guard against green fly and mildew, as the last is apt to appear with the advent of cool nights.

"Early hybrids are apt to be short stemmed, so as soon as you are satisfied the buds are set, give a little higher temperature, about sixty-five at night, which will have a tendency to lengthen out the stem and not injure the flowers, if you gradually reduce the temperature some time before the buds show color. The flowers should open in a night temperature of from fifty to fifty-five; lower than that they do not develop freely.

"Never let the beds get dry after the plants are well covered with foliage, as a bed of healthy hybrids carries a great quantity of large leaves that quickly suffer if the soil become at all dry. Occasionally I find it necessary to use manure water after the buds are set, but only when the plants are not of the right color, or the top dressing appears dried, which will happen if too old when applied.

"After the flowers have been cut from an early house, the plants can be removed and the room occupied with those grown in boxes for the purpose, or they can be dried off for about three weeks, the blind wood removed and started up as before. By this plan you will obtain about half a crop of flowers for Easter. or early spring, when they are still in demand.

"The treatment of later houses will be the same, except the planting need not be done as early, and the drying will not be so tedious, the cool nights helping to check the growth. When starting a house in midwinter, use a little more heat and a little less water.

"The best soil is a rich, free, sandy loam. If too stiff and heavy it is apt to open large cracks, when quite dry, in that way breaking and injuring a great many of the roots; because of this it would be well to use plenty of sand with such a soil.

"The varieties mostly grown around Philadelphia are, Mrs. John Laing, Magna Charta, Uhlrich Brunner, Baroness Rothschild and Madam Gabriel Luizet. Some other varieties are also used, but not in quantity. Baroness Rothschild will not succeed well if brought into flower before the last of February. Mrs. John Laing must not be dried too severely or it will die after being cut back."

CHAPTER XXXI
FLORIST'S GREEN.

This fills such an important place in all cut flower work, especially in connection with roses, this volume would seem incomplete without a short description of such kinds as are most in demand.

For many years smilax was all that could be depended upon for this purpose, but now both ferns and asparagus are largely grown and in many instances by specialists.

Smilax is of exceedingly easy culture, but to be grown to profit, should have under heat and a rich soil about eight inches in depth. If grown more than one year, it should have a rest in July and be started into growth in August by top dressing and watering, and the stringing should be all done before it makes much growth. After the runners begin to push out strong, it should be gone over every few days and pains taken to keep the growth of each plant on its own string. This takes but little time if attended to often, but when neglected a few days causes no end of trouble. When growing rapidly, it will take considerable water, but care should be taken not to have the soil become sodden, neither will it do to let it go for any length of time, without examining to see if the bed is dry at the bottom, as the under heat so necessary to grow a crop quickly, soon dries the nearest roots if not carefully watched. The syringe must be used to keep spider at bay, and for this purpose perfectly clear water should be used, as any sediment, clay or lime deposit will mar the clear glossy surface of the leaves. The usual remedies for the subjugation of green fly must be used, and in the fall when the new crop is growing, grasshoppers must be carefully excluded, as well as constant watch kept for cut worms. These last are very destructive, and sometimes attain a size equal to any seen in cornfields or truck gardens. Two varieties of cut worms are often found,—the dark ones, which as a rule cut the plant at the root; and the lighter brown, that climb the plant and destroy the young shoots. Until recently no means of extermination were thought to be practicable but hand picking. Those that climb and work among the foliage may be easily found by lamplight, and a few nights of careful hunting will rid the bench of them. The others are more difficult to find, but the same course must be pursued, and thorough search made in the soil where one is suspected of being secreted. A more detailed description of the methods of destroying these worms will be found on page 167.

When a crop has nearly made its growth, it may be hardened by a partial withholding of water, commencing with one end and progressing each day as fast as it will be needed when ready to cut. In this way, when cutting commences, it can all be taken, the bed cleaned, mulched, watered and started into a new growth as fast as the first crop is removed. A little liquid manure applied with the water is very beneficial after growth has commenced, and when beds are grown two years, considerable of this will be needed the second year. I would neither divide old roots for replanting, nor grow them more than two seasons. It is better to grow from seed and plant at least every two years, and thus be enabled to furnish a new and unexhausted soil. Young plants should be well grown in four inch pots by the first of August and ready to plant.

Adiantums are also grown in large quantities for this purpose. Of these, cuneatum and gracillimum are used most in connection with cut flower work and respond to the same treatment. It is not necessary to raise seedlings every season, for if properly performed the stocks may be divided several times. This should be done in June. It is preferable to divide to crowns that will go in a three inch pot, removing at the same time all rusty fronds and stumps of former cuttings. If at hand, obtain a part of the soil from some upland locality where wild ferns grow, or leaf mould is to be found. If these are not to be had, chop some sphagnum fine, mix with it flour of bone in the proportion of four quarts to a bushel, using one bushel of sphagnum so mixed, to six of good loam. The soil should be good, but free from anything in the shape of manure that is not thoroughly decomposed, and the manure should be used rather sparingly even then. When these plants have been divided and potted, they should be set on a bench that has been properly shaded, all drafts kept from them, and the house kept warm, damp, and free from the entrance of any air for a few days, or until they commence to make root. When the plants are ready, shift to a five inch pot, and from this size to an eight, which will be the last, and this should be done early in September. Crock the pots well, and for the last shift cover the crocking with a handful of sphagnum through which bone meal has been mixed in the proportion of one to eight. Fill around the ball with soil as first recommended, being careful to settle it with a tamping stick so there shall be no vacancies or loose places. In the spring a little liquid manure in the water once or twice a week will carry them through, being careful not to apply it to them when they are dry. They should be grown in a temperature of from 68° to 70°, no air admitted to the plants direct, but sufficient allowed to escape to keep the house sweet. Shading should be supplied in a way that will be permanent, and for this, common paint is best. If desired to give it a green tinge, it can be easily done, and the effect produced is much the same as seen in their native wilds. Warmth, a moist atmosphere and shade are the three great requisites to a successful growth. Of insect enemies, the snail is the worst, and must be guarded against. Before any plants are put in a house it should be thoroughly scalded, every inch of it, wood work benches and all the soil underneath them, with boiling water. If this is done thoroughly, and snails are not brought in afterwards by means of soil or other methods, but little trouble will be had from them during the entire season. I would not advise the planting of ferns on benches, as they will not produce as many fronds by one third as when treated in the way described.

Asparagus plumosus is largely taking the place of smilax for decorations. Form a solid bed on the ground where plenty of head room can be had, giving tile drainage and a foot of good soil. For the first season's growth, plant as early as you can spare the room, giving it as much of the season as possible, but the same plants will do well for two or three years. After the crop has been cut, if bench room is needed, build a temporary one over it and let it go wild until August 1st, withholding water from it. This gives a natural period of rest. As early as September 1st, clean up, top dress and start into growth, and by December it should have made its growth, been hardened off and be ready for cutting. As a good two year old plant will make from one to three strings, commanding from 50 to 75 cents each, it will readily be seen that this is a paying crop.

CHAPTER XXXII.
THE CARNATION.

In the estimation of most flower lovers, this ranks second only to the rose. The beautiful variegations in color, its delightful fragrance, and good keeping qualities rendering it a favorite with all, and I somewhat doubt if the rose, even, is now claiming as much attention from growers of cut flowers as is this grand flower. Improvements through hybridization during the past few years have been very marked, and to-day buyers are oftentimes at a loss to decide which of the many varieties offered, they shall replace the older ones with.

It is a well established fact that the life of all varieties is comparatively short. Some place the period during which any one variety can be grown to profit, as being limited to five or six years. It is certainly true

—and as we look backward our own experience proves it beyond question—that many well known varieties fail to do as well as at first, some having failed altogether, deterioration going on from year to year until they ceased to be a source of profit and had to be discarded. There is little doubt but that the method of reproduction is largely responsible for this state of things, for the reason that nature designed a period of rest for this plant, but when we find a variety suited to our trade or locality, we usually keep it growing three hundred and sixty-five days in the year, and as many years as its constitutional vigor will sustain it. That the vigor of all plants of this class is greater the nearer they are to the parent seed, the numerous new seedlings now produced every year fully attest. It has come to be a fixed opinion, with those who have given the matter careful study, that so long as plants are renewed from cuttings without rest—which, by the way, it seems almost impossible to give to any extent when propagated in the usual way—just so long will it be necessary to replace the old plants, every few years, with seedlings. Some of our best growers are raising seedlings each year with this end in view, hoping thus to keep the product fully up to the standard in quantity, quality also being increased through ability to keep them in more perfect health. Some varieties show a greater degree of vitality than others, but with few exceptions the tendency downward can be detected early in their career. Careful observation and trial will undoubtedly prove the life of any seedling to be longest when surrounded by all the conditions of soil and climate where it originated. The record of two well known varieties, Buttercup and Grace Wilder, would seem to prove this. The former of these grows luxuriantly in sections near where it originated, while few have any success with it elsewhere. Grace Wilder also is still a favorite in many localities, while in others, notwithstanding it usually makes a fine growth of foliage, the color of bloom—so exquisite in some sections—is badly mottled, rendering it utterly worthless. This would seem to indicate that growers would do well to try new varieties carefully, until they prove to be adapted to their soil and location.

That a seeming necessity exists for a change of stock every few years, none who have given the matter thought will hardly deny, and the carnation grower should carefully test every meritorious variety each year, retaining only such as suit his soil and climate. The large place this plant fills in the world of flowers warrants much more space than can be accorded it here, and if all its various interests were fully treated, it would require a volume of itself. Opinions differ materially among growers in relation to many points in its cultivation, and as these differences of opinion cannot all be given here, the writer can only state the conditions producing success or failure with him. I know of no plant, seemingly of such easy cultivation, that requires more careful study than this, and this fact is coming to be generally recognized more and more each year. So important has it become in the eyes of cultivators, a national society has recently been formed, through means of which, it is hoped, an interchange of thought and experience will result in greatly advancing the interest and value of this general favorite, as well as stimulate all to a closer study of both its nature and needs. This is well, and everyone should avail himself of every means at his command relating to its wants, through intercourse with others, and knowledge of their experience; and still, perhaps more than with any other flower we cultivate, are we at last obliged to fall back upon our own resources. And this, because varieties and conditions which succeed with one fail with another, so there is no certainty without a trial—however popular or perfect a plant may be in one section of the country—of its reproducing itself in these respects in another. It is a study absolutely necessary for each grower to make for himself. Only a few general principles can be laid down as a basis of growth, and some of these must be varied to meet the want produced by variety, soil, or climate.

With the writer, the following conditions have been conducive to the greatest degree of success, though failures have sometimes come where they have been observed; but, as already stated, these failures were due mainly to changing to such varieties as had not been previously proved, but which had succeeded in other localities, and in other soils. My experience has been that cuttings made in December, potted and kept in a temperature of from 50° to 55° until shifted to a two and a half or three-inch pot, gave the best results, as when this shift is given, the centre can be removed, causing eyes to break from the base of the plant, and if allowed to remain in the same temperature until the new roots begin to push, the plants can then be removed to a cold house or frame. This not only relieves benches always needed at that season of the year, but gives the plant a short period of rest, hardens and fits it for being placed in the open ground without injury, as soon as the season opens sufficiently.

Early planting, especially in warm latitudes, is one of the great essentials, otherwise root action will not be well established with the advent of dry or warm weather, rendering the plant liable to a feeble stunted growth. For soil, the best in my opinion for field growth, is an upland light loam that was thoroughly manured the previous season, no fertilizer whatever being used the year of planting, unless it be wood ashes, bone meal, or some known and proved commercial fertilizer that will not increase the dryness of the soil. Plant in squares fourteen by fourteen inches, so they can be worked both ways with a hand cultivator. Care should be had not to plant too deep, and if done early, the ball should be just below the surface, pressed down carefully, leaving a slight depression around the plant. If the season is dry, a light stirring of the soil each day will be of benefit, as will also a slight syringing of the foliage just at night. Topping, as a rule, should cease by the middle of August, but this must be modified by the time bloom is desired, by variety and locality, and is a point for each grower to determine for himself. No frost should ever be allowed to touch them in the fall, though a light frost on acclimated plants in the spring is not harmful. Benches should be well drained, and the soil in them six inches deep. Early out of doors, and early in doors, is the result of my observation, as it gives a strong plant early in the fall for lifting, and one that will soon adapt itself to the new order of growth. Taking one season with another, in all localities north of central Indiana, they should be housed by September 10th. If grown and planted as already recommended, by the first of September the new breaks will have formed from the last topping, the plant will be strong and in a condition to bear transplanting much better than when the blooming stems are well advanced, as in this condition the check given sometimes blasts the first buds. For this class of plants, and at this season of the year, provided the soil from which they are taken and to which they are to be removed is similar in character, lifting carefully with a ball is far preferable to shaking out clean, as may safely be done with smaller plants. A preservation of all the roots should be sought first, and as much of the ball supporting them as can be handled conveniently, second. The distance at which they should be planted in a bench depends upon the growth they have made in the field, as well as to the length of time they are to remain in the house. In either case, they must not be so close that air cannot circulate freely among them. Never plant them any deeper in the bench than they were grown in the field, or they are liable to decay at the base and their usefulness be destroyed.

The method of planting depends upon the way it is desired to support them, and this supporting should be

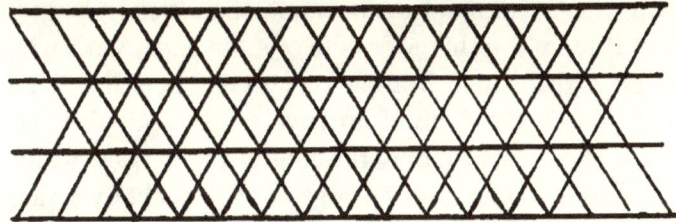

Fig. 33.

done as soon as planted. If the plants of a row are so arranged as to come between those of the preceding row, they can be supported best by wires running lengthwise of the bed, interlaced with string running across them. To do this, stretch rows of No. 16 galvanized wire from end to end of the bench, ten inches apart and six inches above the soil. Support these by light wooden cross pieces every twenty feet. Take common white cord, and instead of running at right angles with the first wire, carry it across the bed diagonally, passing the ball around each wire as you proceed. The distance between the strings should be six inches, and when finished the surface will be as represented in Fig. 33. Two men, one on each side of a bench, will perform the work rapidly.

The plants will soon grow up through this net work and it will prevent their being pressed to the ground by the weight of additional growth. For strong plants my preference is for wire netting. Take a roll of two inch mesh chicken-wire, cut in lengths the width of the bench, divide this into two pieces, lengthwise, fasten each edge to oak or yellow pine strips one inch by half inch with small staples one-fourth of an inch in length. A still more durable way is to sew the edges with wire to five-eighths inch iron rods of suitable length. Bend this now in the form of an inverted V, and place between the rows, fastening the ends of the strips to which the wire is fastened to the edge of the bench, by means of common staples. This will commend itself to all who adopt it, for the following reasons: It keeps all foliage from touching the ground at any time during the season; a constant current of air passes through the space caused by the inverted V, drying out any dampness that may have gathered; liquid food can easily be supplied without wetting the foliage, and when the season is over, shut one into another, they occupy but little space, can quickly be placed in position when wanted, and will last for years if properly cared for.

Early in-door planting requires watchfulness as well as the best of facilities for keeping down the temperature. To grow carnations successfully, abundant ventilation must be provided both in the roof, at the ends and in both walls, and for this reason houses used for them should never join each other. Build to obtain the greatest amount of sunlight, but above all, provide all the ventilation possible. The soil in which they are planted should not be made as firm as described for roses, but left loose enough to be able to plant with the hand, after which, water well. For the first week shade with a clay wash, put on every inch of air possible, and if very warm, syringe the foliage with a fine spray as often as it becomes dry, being careful not to saturate the soil. Root action under these conditions will commence at once, and no matter how hot it is, your plants will in a week forget that they were ever moved. The average night temperature in which carnations should be grown for flowering, is fifty-six, but varies with varieties, some requiring more, some less. It also depends upon the use to which the plants are to be put. If it is to fill up space that will be wanted for other purposes after the first crop is off, they should be cut back in the field with this end in view. In this case the night temperature can be a few degrees higher, but all plants which you desire should bloom from November to July must be given a lower temperature; nor will it do to deprive them to any extent of their foliage. I consider this a fruitful source of some of the obstacles we meet to-day, and shall have occasion to refer to it again under the head of the diseases to which this plant is susceptible. It will have been observed by those acquainted with carnations, that the conditions most suitable to their development in the open air, are to be found in the month of September. It is then they make the most rapid as well as healthy growth, and if we would obtain the most perfect success it is well for us to study nature's methods during the month spoken of. At this season of the year the days are usually warm but the nights cool, and in the latter part of the month, mercury often indicates forty. I do not believe in growing carnations cool, as it is termed, if that means the thermometer should never be allowed to rise above sixty during the day if it can be kept that low. September days are warm, and from this we may conclude warmth with plenty of air is not injurious, and if the temperature remains at sixty during the evening, gradually falling from that during the night, even to forty, it is much more in accord with the condition of things in the month referred to, than to aim to keep a low temperature both day and night. While a mean degree is given at fifty-six, there is no doubt but that variations during the twenty-four hours of from seventy-five at noon to forty or forty-five at four in the morning, are more in accord with natural conditions, at the season of the year in which they do the best in the field.

The soil, if it be a sandy loam sod, may be made as strong as one part of manure to five of soil, but it is imperative that the manure be so thoroughly decomposed and mixed through the soil, as to render its presence difficult of detection. Bone meal and wood ashes are also good, but to be available as food, should be incorporated with the soil pile when made, and this should be several months in advance of the time when it will be needed, in order to have it thoroughly decomposed, as the structure of carnation roots is fine, and they are impatient of any coarse or green material. When necessary to supply food during their period of flowering, if the dirt has settled so the top has fallen below the balls of the plants, a light mulching between the rows will be of benefit, otherwise it is easiest to supply what is needed in a liquid state, but it is always better to supply this in small doses and often, than to give it in any abundance. Some growers supply a little with the water every time it is applied to the soil. For a change from the usual forms, aqua ammonia is good, and if used should not exceed one pint to two barrels of water, and in this strength no fears need be entertained of injury to the plants, even though used quite often. As in the feeding of roses, it is well to rotate liquids, but care must be taken not to give them more than they can assimilate.

One of the most congenial forms of food is to be found in spent hops. These must never be used in the green state, but should be at least a year old before they are fit for plant food, and if exposed to the air and weather for two years, so much the better. When brought from the brewery they should not be piled more than three feet deep, and turned often in order not to have them fire-fang. When all danger of this is passed, they can be brought together in more compact form, and turned occasionally until wanted for use. I would not advise mixing them with the soil, but have had excellent success when they have been used on the bottom of a bench. Before filling with soil, spread evenly over the whole surface a coat from an inch to one and a half inches deep, and let the roots seek them when they wish. Eventually they will be completely matted with roots if a proper degree of moisture is given. Some of the finest and most prolific plants I have ever grown were the result of this treatment.

When it is desired to bloom a house of carnations the entire season, the night temperature should not exceed 55° during the winter months, nor should any foliage be taken from the plants. As the power of the sun increases in the spring, a light shading should be applied to the glass. Keep all weeds removed, and early in March apply a mulching two inches deep. The manure used for this purpose should be a year old.

For spider and green fly, both spraying and fumigating must be attended to, but never syringe in the latter part of the day, or allow any dampness to be present on the foliage as night approaches. Some of our finest varieties, in order to make first-class flowers, need to be disbudded. This also each grower must regulate in accordance with the requirement of his market. Varieties change so often, and there are so many in cultivation, it does not seem best to occupy space here in an endeavor to describe their individual treatment, and in this connection I will only speak of Buttercup, as up to the present time it is the best of its color, and comparatively few succeed with it. More than usual care should be exercised to have every cutting in perfect health when taken from the plant. These should be rooted, and treated as previously described, as they are more difficult to propagate after January. In the field they can be planted in a good loam, but for bench work they need a stiffer soil than other varieties, and I have had the best success on south benches and where under heat was abundant. Propagate and grow twice the number you wish to flower, and when housing never allow any plants to come inside that have the slightest indication of anything but the most perfect health.

The chief insect enemies, aside from those mentioned, are slugs, mice, twitter and cut worms. Slugs and snails will be conspicuous by their absence if the house has been thoroughly scalded before being planted.

Mice are often very destructive and must be disposed of by trapping, or by poison. Twitter is caused by a small insect similar to the green fly—so says Prof. Baker—and the remedies effectual with that, are with this also. Their presence becomes known when the leaves are seen to curl, and the shoot curve as though it had been stung. For a remedy in the field, kerosene emulsion is recommended by the same authority. Not having been troubled with it since knowing what it was, I have not had occasion to try this remedy. Cut worms work on the buds, cutting a small hole through its case and eating off the petals at their juncture with its base. Their work is done at night, secreting themselves in the soil, under anything on its surface, or among the foliage at the base of the plant as soon as dawn appears. The appearance of cut worms among carnations is comparatively new, and the writer has been afflicted with their presence but once, in the winter of '92. The fact that only one variety was attacked by them, although there was another in the same house, led to the conclusion the eggs must have been deposited on the plants while in the field, as no others were affected, nor were other carnations grown in the same part of the field as those upon which the worms were found. When their depredations are first noticed, they should be attended to at once, or every bud is liable to be destroyed in a short time. In the instance referred to, but little attention was paid to them at first, the carnations were removed when the bench was needed, a little sand spread over the soil and the bench filled with plants of Meteor in five inch pots. After these had been there a short time, it was noticed something was at work on the foliage, but no worms were found at first, but in a short time they had grown so rapidly that in two nights they nearly stripped the plants of foliage. A search among the pots unearthed nearly a quart two-thirds grown, on a bench of seven hundred square feet. Although no opportunity has been given to try it, I feel confident a dose of vaporized extract applied at night would exterminate them. Mr. Lombard, a large grower in Massachusetts, recommends Dalmation powder in about the proportion of one pound to 1,000 plants, dusting it all over the foliage. He states he has tried it for both carnations and smilax, with the result that large quantities were killed, and that three applications rid the place of them.

Carnation blooms are benefited by keeping the stems in water in a cool place a few hours before placing them on the market. If you would establish a reputation for first-class flowers, careful attention must be given to every detail connected with their growth. Keep pace with the times by proving varieties that take high rank elsewhere, and if adapted to your soil, be in a condition to compete with others for the patronage of your section. As the cut flower business is conducted now, it is the man who keeps both eyes and ears open to what is going on around him, who reaps profit from his investment. Study carefully all the peculiarities of both plant and soil. Allow no flowers to go on the market until fully developed, and thus increase both size and value. Above all, do not place first and second-class flowers together. Bunch the latter by themselves or discard them altogether, the others will bring more money, even if their number is considerably less. As fast as a variety ceases to do as well with you as in former years, no matter how great a favorite it has been, substitute for it new and younger blood from among the varieties you have tested, and that have proved to be adapted to your locality.

CHAPTER XXXIII.
DISEASES OF THE CARNATION.

The subject of the various diseases to which this plant is liable, is being made a careful study by men well qualified for this particular line of investigation. Much has already been revealed by these researches, much also is yet to be discovered as to prevention and cure. No doubt exists in my mind but what the disease denominated the "yellows" in former years, was caused to a great extent through exhausted vitality. The plant had served its day and generation, had been grown without cessation, and either died of premature old age or became so debilitated as to fall an easy prey to some of the diseases about which we then knew so little. I remember also that some years since, when living where land was scarce, this trouble was more frequent among plants grown for two or more years upon the same ground. An experience of many years with various species of plants, has convinced me that almost without exception, health and vigor are best preserved when a system of rotation is strictly adhered to. I do not believe the carnation is an exception to the general rule, but on the contrary, that disease is less liable to attack plants full of vigor, and that this vigor is increased when the plants are grown in fresh soil each season.

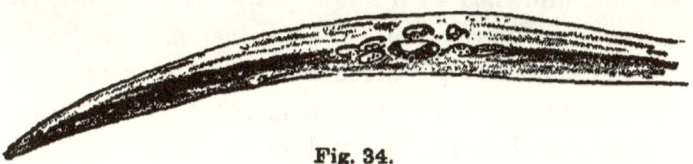

Fig. 34.

Rust, a later and very dangerous enemy, scientists tell us is a fungus, and spreads with great rapidity. It is only within a few days that the writer has seen this pest, and from what little was seen of it then, he became convinced it was a disease every grower should take the utmost precaution to avoid. There is no doubt but that it is highly contagious, and if once seen, vigorous measures should be taken to stamp it out. It first appears on the leaves in form of small brown spots. These are raised above the surface and will rub off and discolor the hand when it is passed over them.

Prof. Arthur, of Purdue University, describes this very fully in a paper read before the American Carnation Society at Buffalo, in 1892, from which I make the following extract:

"Rust has long been known in Europe, and is especially common in Italy and Germany. The first impression that it was brought from Europe in the importation of 1891 is found to be erroneous, it having been found by Prof. Taft, of Lansing, Mich., in 1890, and was known in some places along the Hudson River three years previous. So far as present information goes, the distribution of carnation rust in America has been accomplished within four years. It is now known to occur in Massachusetts, Pennsylvania, New York, Ohio, Michigan and Indiana, and a few infected centres might distribute the rust by means of rooted cuttings, as widely as there is a demand for the flowers.

"A precautionary measure, after rust has appeared in a house, is to keep the air as cool and dry as is compatible with the health of the plants, thus retarding the growth and distribution of the spores.

"Wherever the rust has obtained much headway, and especially where it appears shortly after the plants have been housed in the fall, the use of some fungicide is almost imperative."

The full text of this paper may be found in Vol. 7,

page 587 of the American Florist. Another illustrated paper from the pen of Prof. Atkinson, of Cornell University, may also be found in Vol. 8, No. 247, of the same publication. The main thing is to avoid rust by being careful not to import upon the place any diseased plants, as well as to use preventive measures, and not wait for the disease to develop and have to burn the crop.

Mr. Ward, a large grower in the state of New York, recommends the following treatment:

CURATIVE AGENCIES USED—Bordeaux Mixture Dry, Bordeaux Mixture Liquid, Ammonia Solution and Fostite.

FORMULA—Dry Bordeaux.—Dissolve 4 lbs. sulphate of copper in two gallons boiling water. Dry slack two bushels of quick lime with the copper solution. The lime must be dry powder after slacking.

BORDEAUX MIXTURE—Liquid.—Dissolve 6 lbs. sulphate of copper in two gallons boiling water and let cool. Mix one peck quick lime in six gallons water and let cool and mix the two solutions. Pour same into a kerosene barrel containing 40 gallons water and stir while using.

AMMONIA SOLUTION.—Two quarts ammonia in which dissolve one pound sulphate of copper, and pour this solution in 20 or 30 gallons of water.

TREATMENT.

DIPPING.—All young plants are immersed in the liquid Bordeaux mixture when set in the open ground. All mature plants are immersed (tops only, not the roots) in the same mixture when benching in.

SPRAYING.—All young plants are sprayed with either the liquid Bordeaux or ammonia solution once in two weeks while under glass, and all field plants are sprayed the same in field.

172   How to Grow Cut Flowers.

Fostite.—Under glass all plant houses are blown full of Fostite in a fine cloud every dark, cloudy day.

Dry Bordeaux is sprinkled over all paths and under all benches every two months.

Fig. 35.

DISEASES OF THE CARNATION. 173

These precautionary measures it is well to adopt if there is the least suspicion of the presence of the disease. If it should appear, avoid using water on the foliage save in the distribution of the solution, and remove and burn all affected plants at once.

The other diseases to which the carnation is subject are: Leaf spot (Septoria), as shown in Fig 35. Anthracnose, as seen in Fig. 36, and Bacterial disease shown in Fig. 37. These engravings were used in illustrating the papers read before the Carnation Society at Pittsburgh in February of the present year by Professors Atkinson and Halstead. A fuller description of the engravings will be found in those papers as published.

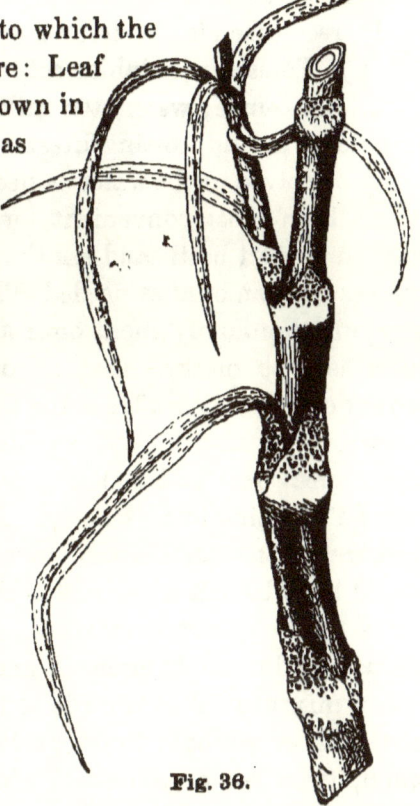

Fig. 36.

By these illustrations readers will be able to recognize the different forms of disease as they may develop, without the detailed description so clearly given in the pages referred to. The practical question which arises is, how shall these diseases be avoided, or if they appear, what is the remedy. In answer to this last question Prof. Halstead, who has given this matter careful study, recommends the following formulas:

"(1.) Potassium sulphide solution: Potassium sulphide, one ounce; water, ten gallons. The potassium sulphide is a solid, costing fifteen cents a pound, and is easily dissolved in the water as needed. In some cases it has been most convenient for me to dissolve the solid in a quart bottle and ask the gardener to pour out the required amount as needed. The application is by spraying thoroughly about once a week. The results have been so marked that in one instance a large grower of carnations after using this mixture for a season wrote me that he felt confident that it had saved him a great deal and that if generally used it would prove a blesssing to all who are affected with carnation diseases of the sorts above mentioned. Possibly it would be of benefit when rust is the leading enemy.

"(2.) The Bordeaux mixture. Perhaps the best fungicide now in use in orchard and garden is the Bordeaux mixture. This is made as follows: Copper sulphate, three pounds; lime (unslacked), two pounds; water, twenty-two gallons. Dissolve the sulphate of copper in one vessel and slack the lime in another,

DISEASES OF THE CARNATION. 175

then mix the two and dilute to the required strength. This is the so-called half-strength Bordeaux mixture which has, in many instances, during the past season, proved as effective as the full strength, and for car-

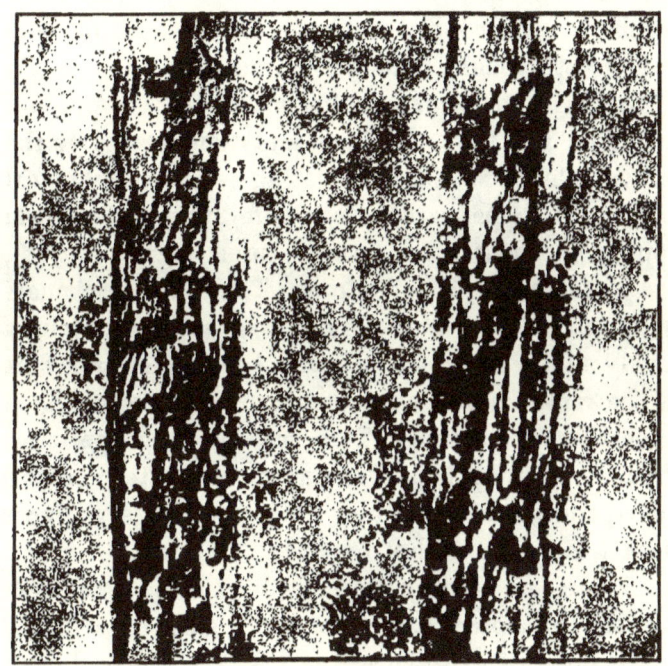

Fig. 37.

nations will be strong enough. It is seen that this is a lime mixture and the foliage will be covered with a bluish white layer. But it is to be remembered that this does not differ greatly from the natural color of the carnation leaf and stem, and it is one that can be quickly removed from the portion sent to market. A weekly spraying of the plants with this Bordeaux mixture should prove remunerative in houses troubled with fungous enemies. The Bordeaux mixture is inexpensive, the copper sulphate (blue vitriol or blue stone) costing eight cents per pound.

"(3.) The ammoniacal solution: A third compound that does not have the lime and therefore gives the sprayed plants no marked coating is the ammoniacal solution of copper carbonate. Its formula is as follows: Copper carbonate, five ounces; aqua ammonia (26), five pints; water, fifty gallons. The copper carbonate is first mixed with water into a paste and the ammonia slowly added until the solution becomes clear. This can be kept in a bottle and the required amount diluted as desired for spraying. The carbonate of copper costs thirty-five cents a pound and ammonia sixteen cents a quart, and therefore enough for spraying a large house weekly is a small bill of expense.

"Taking all things into consideration it is probable that the three preparations above described are arranged in the order of excellence, the best being placed last."

The disease called anthracnose, is better known by florists as "the cutting bed fungus." This is the form so destructive at times to cuttings when in the sand. Hard wooded cuttings are often blackened by it, but its ravages are greatest among the more tender kinds among which is the carnation, and it is not unusual to find large numbers destroyed in a single night. Until quite recently nothing has been known that would keep this in check.

The remedy I am now using for this form of fungus is similar to Prof. Halstead's No. 3, and is 1 lb. of the sulphate of copper dissolved in 2 qts. of ammonia. In wetting down the sand before the cuttings are put in, use one pint of the solution in 60 gallons of water. Should any signs of fungus appear while the cuttings are in the sand, sprinkle them lightly with a solution made by adding one ounce of the original solution to a common can of water.

One other form of disease described by Professor Halstead he calls "Rosette." So far as my observation extends, this is seen in Buttercup more frequently than in any other variety. Instead of growing so freely in the field as to need topping, the plant affected rarely throws up a flowering shoot. It seems to be dwarfed, and although clothed with the usual amount of foliage, this is so close jointed as to present the form suggested by the name Rosette. The first thing noticeable about these plants is their color. Instead of retaining the beautiful dark green of perfect health, they gradually turn to a lighter hue, and if left to themselves either remain stunted through the season, or die.

I think it extremely doubtful if any remedy will reach and cure this form of disease. The best way is to remove them root and branch at once, and burn them. No plants should ever be removed from the field to a flowering bench that show the least traces of this disease, and if it appears, as it sometimes will, on seemingly healthy plants after removal to the house, drastic measures should at once be adopted.

The first impression produced by a careful examination of the illustrated papers previously referred to, on these various diseases, is, that with such an array of forces opposed to success, the fight is an unequal one, and the odds greatly against us. Be that as it may, it is a plain case of conquering or of being conquered, and while it is well to use every means at our command for overcoming and eradicating disease when present, ought we not to look for preventive, rather than curative, agencies? Have we not been violating some of nature's laws, and thus weakened the resisting power of our plants.

I am firmly convinced that a radical change must take place in the cultivation of the carnation if we would preserve its flowering properties. In true American style we have rushed this plant, as we do every thing else we think we see any money in, and in so doing have nearly doubled the time nature designed it to be in active working condition.

We claim that exhausted vitality must be restored through the medium of healthy seedlings. After we have obtained these, what do we do? Plant a bench or a house with them, try to mature fine show blooms, at the same time stripping the plants of every cutting that can be obtained for sale. Disease is thus invited, and I think that cases in which the invitation is not quickly responded to, will be found to be the exception. Two instances of this kind have come under my observation within twelve months, one of them upon my own place. The varieties in question were very strong growing two year old seedlings, apparently in perfect health. The treatment given them was such as has just been described, and resulted in both instances in a bad case of the spot disease, while other varieties within the same walls, treated in a more humane manner, gave no indication of its presence.

While the removal of a few cuttings from healthy plants that produce them in abundance may be no injury, yet as a rule such as are set apart for flowering, especially if cut with long stems, should be given all the foliage with which nature surrounds them.

Again it would be more in the line of natural conditions could we give our young plants a longer period of rest. This can only be done by planting for this special purpose in the spring, taking out the bloom buds, and from the laterals which form, propagate the stock for next season's planting. This should be done early enough to have them rooted and boxed, ready to set away in a cool place, as soon as cold weather comes. In this way, from three to four months of rest can be given them.

Still another method is to grow the plants as before described, but not to remove the bloom buds until time to take up the plants. They should then be potted, and after roots have formed, the plants should be kept in a dormant state during the winter. Whenever the cuttings are wanted, the plants can be brought into a warm house and the laterals will soon form. This is the only way in which perfect rest can be given and at the same time have young spring struck cuttings for field planting.

If a similar system were to be pursued with winter grown cuttings offered for sale, it would greatly lessen the danger we so much desire to avoid. On these no flowers should be allowed to mature. As soon as the bud fairly appears, break it off, removing with it such laterals as throw bloom, and from the rest make the desired stock, leaving the foliage at the base of the plant for its support. The plants should also be grown in a temperature somewhat below the average.

The objection which will be raised by growers to this method, is its expense. Two or three times as much would have to be paid for cuttings as they can now be obtained for, in order to make it remunerative, but would it not be to the interest of the buyer to insist upon this class of stock and be willing to pay a fair price for it, rather than to risk the income from an entire crop upon a cheaper grade? It goes without saying that carnation growers will be willing to give us whatever we are willing to pay for, but in the present headlong race for trade the price of rooted carnation cuttings has fallen below that at which a first-class article can be produced.

CHAPTER XXXIV.
CHRYSANTHEMUMS.

The first question for the cut flower grower to decide is, not how many he shall grow, or in what form he shall grow them, but shall he grow any. Will the market upon which I depend for their sale, consume the crop at prices that will compensate me for the labor? Another query must also be answered while this is under consideration. If a house is devoted to them, what crops will follow that can be disposed of, and that will consume the space without loss of time? The amount of bloom placed on the market each season, by those who plant and gather it in much the same way they would sow and reap a sheaf of grain, and with as little care, is appalling. If this is the only class of bloom your market will take, it is better to leave their cultivation to others, saving what little of time and strength would be expended on them, for other things.

If on the other hand the taste of the consumer in your vicinity has been educated to look for, and be willing to pay for a better article, no one who grows and sells his own product without the intervention of middlemen, will need to hesitate long as to the form in which they are to be grown or as to what shall succeed them. The demand will regulate the form, and on all retail places there are many ways of supplying a crop to occupy the vacant space. With the commercial grower, the matter of succession must be decided before commencing. If your market will take a crop of Harrisii lilies for Easter, or of hybrids that have been grown through the summer in boxes, then a crop of chrysanthemums will add materially to the income to be derived from a house, as either of the above can then be followed by a crop of teas or hybrids for the season following, and no time will be lost.

When the market demands well grown sprays, the cuttings should be made in April, potted, topped once, shifted, and planted in the bench in June twelve inches each way, and the first shoots pinched out once only. As they grow, all weak wood should be removed, and the buds on those allowed to mature, thinned to the number of blooms desired in a spray. This method will not give as strong or straight stems as when each plant is allowed to mature but one spray. When grown in the last named form the cuttings may be made and the planting done two or three weeks later. When grown to single stem the top should never be removed, but every facility given the plants to make straight stems by staking them at the proper time.

CHRYSANTHEMUMS.

They can also be more easily cared for when the rows across a bench are 12 inches apart, but the plants constituting the row may be six inches apart.

Again, if single flowers on long stems are desired, soft cuttings should be rooted by the first of July, and planted as soon as ready from a two inch pot, in four inches of soil, six inches by 12, as before described. Care should be taken to plant the low growing varieties where there is the least amount of head room. If they are to be supported by wire stakes, the upper wires should be in position before the bench is planted.

The soil should be composed of two-thirds decayed sod of a rather light texture, and one-third well composted manure, to which add fifty lbs of flour of bone to the amount of soil necessary for a hundred foot house. Give them plenty of air without drafts. See that they never lack for water, or receive a check of any kind from the time the cutting is made, until the bloom is perfected. Remove all laterals as fast as they appear, and as soon as the buds are formed, remove all but one. This should usually be the crown, but if that is in any way imperfect, select the best one. From this time until the flowers show color, liquid manure should be supplied liberally, but not too strong, or when the soil is in the least dry. In whatever portion of the house your highest colors are planted, see that the glass is shaded slightly, or the full sunlight will fade the bloom.

When flowers are grown for exhibition purposes, the plants should be given more room, at least 10x12 inches.

Some prefer planting 12 inches each way when growing for single blooms, the plants being rooted in April, and pinched back twice, giving in this way three or four individual flowers and stems to a plant. The same objection is met in this method as when they are grown for sprays, the crooked stem lessens their value.

Exhibition flowers, or such as it is desired to keep a week or more, should be cut just before they are fully developed, placed in water immediately, and set on a cool, light cellar bottom. Each morning the water should be changed and the stems freshened by cutting a thin slice from the ends.

It does not properly come within the province of this work, to treat of growing pot plants for exhibition purposes, but it may not be amiss to speak of growing single flowers in small pots, as some may desire to grow a few in this way, who cannot devote a house to them.

The cuttings should be made the last of June. Particular care should be taken to see that each pot has a good sized hole for drainage. When they need a shift, they should be changed from a two inch to a four inch pot and matured in that size. As soon as they need it, supply them with a neat stake of sufficient length to confine the plant to as it grows. Great care must be taken not to let them become dry in the least. On hot or windy days, examine them every hour. Keep them inside through the entire season, encouraging them by every possible means to make as rapid a growth as is consistent with sturdy vigor. Use weak liquid manure water every day. Keep all laterals removed, and just as the buds begin to show, strew a liberal sprinkling of flour of bone on the sand on which they stand. As soon as the bud that is to remain is selected, and the others are removed, handle and size them, giving to each plant three inches of space each way, and place them where they are to remain *without being disturbed again* until the flower is perfected. It will be but a few days before the roots will go through the bottom of the pot and spread out like a fan in search of the bone. This will cause the plants to produce flowers of enormous size compared with the amount of pot room given to the roots, and when placed where the size of the pot and bloom can be compared, beholders are filled with wonder and amazement at the result. Of course they are in blissful ignorance as to the cause, but that does not warrant any one in saying it is a trick. There are no tricks in our business. They were all appropriated by the trades which preceded us. If it is desired to exhibit any of these in pots, the roots should be severed that are outside of them, and in doing this no harm will result to the blooms if they have matured, and if they are kept liberally supplied with water.

Changes are taking place yearly through the introduction of new seedlings, some of which prove superior to existing varieties of the same shade. For this reason no list can be given which can be expected to stand intact for many years, but the following are some of those best adapted to growing for cut flowers, and the future will have to produce a more perfect list, before these will be supplanted:

Joseph H. White, Ivory, Minnie Wanamaker, Flora Hill, Niveus, for white. For yellow, H. E. Wiedner, Golden Wedding, W. H. Lincoln. Pink—Vivian Morel, Mermaid, Ada Spalding.

The chrysanthemum has always been considered as healthy and rugged as a weed, but experiences of the past year prove that this plant also is liable to disease. Eel worms have been found in the roots in sections where they have infested the rose. If there is any indication of their being present in either the soil or manure used for chrysanthemums, the same measures of prevention should be adopted as described for the treatment of soil used for roses.

In the fall of 1892, a new fungoid disease attacked a bed of chrysanthemums that were being grown for cut flowers. The plants were in a vigorous state of growth at the time, and the gentleman under whose care they were, states that they were treated with the usual fungicides but without avail. Mr. Dearness thus describes the disease:

"The fungus can be easily recognized by the dark

blotches, usually about half to three-quarters of in inch in diameter. In these blotches are found the spore heaps or pits and beyond them the leaf turns yellow; not long afterwards the whole leaf shrivels and is drawn downward to the stem.

"As the hyphæ of this fungus grow through the tissue of the leaf it cannot be easily reached by external applications. Doubtless the best course is to burn the affected leaves or destroy the plant as soon as the disease is observed."

Another grower of the chrysanthemum tells me he observed the same disease on some imported plants at about the same time as those just described. These he removed at once and burned them. Evidently this was accomplished before the spores had time to ripen and spread, as he saw no indications of the disease afterwards. The experience of these two growers shows us conclusively, that we cannot be too watchful, and that great care must be taken if the disease is once discovered, to stamp it out immediately.

The black aphis so troublesome to the chrysanthemum is more tenacious of life than the common green fly. If the usual fumigation does not destroy it, the plants should be syringed with a strong decoction of tobacco water.

CHAPTER XXXV.

VIOLETS.

The amount of capital invested in the production of the violet, while seemingly small, is in the aggregate a large sum. True, the greater part of it is represented by labor, but in some states and localities much time is devoted to its cultivation. In its native home the winters are mild, and here it is found at its best in a night temperature of from forty-five to fifty. Any attempt towards forcing this sweet scented flower through the application of heat, immediately defeats the object sought, and natural changes of temperature that come with the advent of spring, tend to gradually lessen the formation of buds, and at the same time encourage in their place an output of new foliage as the temperature incident to the change is raised. Since the advent a few years since of the disease which has proved so destructive in some localities, much discussion has arisen in relation to the propagation and growth of the plants, some claiming their vitality was lessened, and their liability to disease increased, by a division of the parent stool at the expiration of the flowering season. However this may be, it is the system I have always practiced, and I have never been troubled with the disease. This leads me to the belief that the disease is communicated rather than produced, and that if none has ever appeared, and no interchange of plants brings it on the place, it is immaterial whether the new plants are made in September from cuttings, or by a division of both the old and new growth in spring. In either case the young plants should be potted and kept cool until the ground can be worked in early spring, when they should be planted. The soil should be in a good state of cultivation, and if that removed from the rose houses is spread one or two inches deep and worked into the beds where violets are to be planted, it will be beneficial to them. The distance at which they should be planted depends upon the amount of land at one's disposal, and the mode of cultivation it is desired to adopt. If for a wheel hoe, fourteen inches each way will be sufficient; if by a horse cultivator, eight inches in the row by three feet between. All runners should be removed during the season of growth, but discrimination must be made between thin runners and the formation of new crowns, and by September there should be from four to eight of these bud producers surrounding the original plant. Many living south of the snow line prefer to flower them in frames, chiefly because the preparation for doing so can be made at less expense, but in all parts of the north the great inconvenience attending their protection from frost in frames, the regulation of temperature, as well as largely increased labors through heavy falls of snow, render house cultivation the more desirable method. Houses ten feet wide facing the south, with roof of equal span, and a walk in the centre, are much used. This form of building depends upon location.

The farther north we go, the more desirable it is to bring the plants as near the glass as possible. Where a wall of suitable height is available, a "lean to" can be added that will accomplish the end sought, but the ordinary south walls of houses built for other purposes are so low, the roof for an addition of this kind must necessarily be rather flat, and head room obtained by excavating a path along the wall is not desirable. Both of these methods are open to objections and are unsatisfactory.

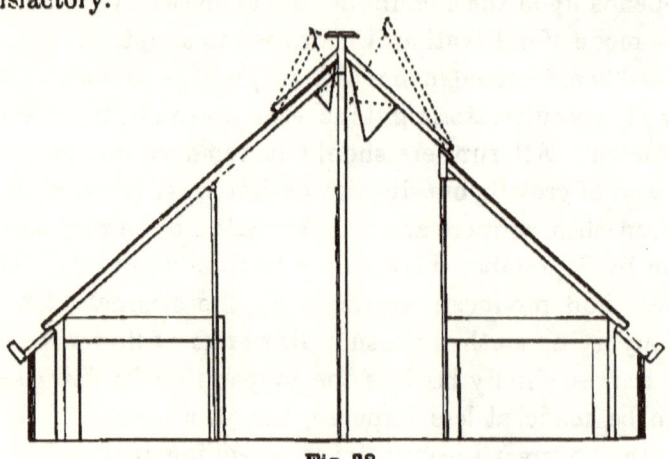

Fig. 38.

If the room can be utilized, an excellent plan is to build an equal span roof twelve feet wide, using the north part for propagating and the south bench for violets. (See Fig. 38.) In this case it will be found advantageous to support each roof with purlins and posts made of one inch gas pipe, in order to use as little wood and as much glass as possible. Winter propagation will also be facilitated by the use of twenty inches or more of glass in the partition wall through the centre of the house, and if permanent sunlight is not wanted through this, it can easily be excluded by a light coat of white paint, serving all the purpose of ground glass. For the north roof, continuous ventilation formed by sash wide enough to receive a twenty inch glass will be sufficient, and this should be protected by a cap projecting from the ridge to exclude gusts of air. The south one should also be continuous, and both should open at the top. In addition to this, if the part of the roof over the south bench is made of movable sash, and the joints between them capped by half-round battens, every other sash, or as many as may be desired, can be so constructed as to add to the ventilation on warm days by simply sliding them down the distance wanted. To do this the upright side of the gutter must be dispensed with. If it is desired, the sash on the south roof can be removed in the spring, the soil taken out, and the bench supplied with new soil and young plants, which can be grown where they are to remain for the winter. This presents many advantages, not the least of which is the avoidance of all danger from the blasting of the buds by removal in the fall.

If plants are grown in the field during summer, the benches should be provided with rich loamy soil, to which it is best to remove the plants before severe frosts prevail. By this time, if the plants have been carefully attended to through the summer, the crowns should be full of buds. To avoid injury to these, after cleaning of all dead leaves and runners, they should be lifted with as much adhering dirt as will save the fibrous roots, and planted in soil sufficiently deep to cover the balls of earth, watered and shaded for a few days until root action commences. A convenient form of shading is by the use of cloth manufactured for the purpose. Fastened to light frames, this can also be used for covering them with at night until time to put on the sash permanently. From the time it is necessary to put on the sash in the fall, until the plants are through flowering in the spring, they need constant care. Do not think because they flourish in a cool atmosphere that heat can be shut off two-thirds of the time and that this is all that they need. Ventilation must be attended to almost as thoroughly as for roses, giving all the air consistent with the outside temperature on bright sunny days, less on cloudy days, but enough to keep the house at from sixty to sixty-five, with a night temperature of from forty-five to forty-eight. They should be cleaned of runners as fast as they appear, as well as leaves which have passed their usefulness. In case there should be an excess of foliage, some of it should be thinned out. Some growers claim the foliage should be seldom if ever wet, believing it has a tendency to spread disease if any is present, but spider must be kept in check, and enough water should be applied to accomplish this.

VIOLETS.

For several years the violet has been a prey to two forms of disease which have nearly exterminated it in some sections. One of these is caused by the same worm which is making so much trouble among roses in some sections. Violet root galls (See Fig. 39), Dr. Halstead tells us, are identical with the lobes found in rose roots.

It would be well to adopt the same precautionary measures for violets as were recommended for roses when nematoids are present in the soil.

Carefully examine the roots when the plants are lifted in the field, and reject all that show any indication of their presence.

The other form of disease, known to growers as leaf spot, is due to a fungus, so says the same authority. Of these, many forms exist, and several may be present on the plant at the same time.

Fig. 39.

Much has been written in relation to this disease during the past three years, both as to cause and remedy. As very few writers agree as to the one producing cause of this trouble, it is reasonable to suppose that several combined may have a direct bearing in the production of this particular form of disease, to which the violet seems to be peculiarly susceptible. Among the various causes assigned are the following: Impaired vitality, springing from the plants being grown in too high a temperature, and propagated while in that condition; an exhaustion, through long years of cultivation, of properties in the soil essential to their growth; extreme atmospheric changes, and the presence of either water or dew on the foliage during the summer. One large grower plants in frames, where they are to remain summer and winter, carefully protecting the plants from dew in the fall by means of canvass shutters. Another plants in the same way, but prevents any water from touching the foliage by means of raised and shaded sash placed two feet over them. In this instance water is applied between the rows as is needed, and spider kept at bay by an occasional syringing in the evening with water in which a small quantity of soap has been boiled, the temperature of the water when applied not being less than 100°. The same method is pursued in winter, save that while the plants are in flower the soap is omitted, and the syringing necessary to keep spider at bay is made with clear water of the same temperature, 100°.

MIGNONETTE.

No remedy has yet been found that will entirely cure this disease when once it takes possession. Air slacked lime is used by some as a preventive, both plants and soil being dusted with it. Mr. Richard Donovan, a successful grower of the violet near Chicago, recommends the use of the ammonia solution in the following proportions: Three oz. of the carbonate of copper dissolved in one qt. of ammonia. Use one gill to three gallons of water, and apply to the foliage by means of a syringe once a week. This will not eradicate the disease, but if applied as soon as any indications of it are seen, it will do much towards holding it in check.

Were it not for these diseases, the flowers would be so abundant there would be no market for them. As it is, a scarcity is caused, and he who succeeds is reasonably sure of being able to dispose of his crop to advantage.

CHAPTER XXXVI.
MIGNONETTE.

For winter cutting, the first care is to obtain good seed. The giant varieties used for this purpose are not always reliable, and it is a much safer way for each grower to raise his own seed. after once obtaining a strain suited to his trade.

When it is desired to grow this in quantity, the best success will be obtained in a span roof house with solid beds on either side of the walk. Continuous ventilation should be supplied in the same way as described for carnations. Good drainage should also be provided for the beds, after which from 18 to 20 inches of rich light soil should be filled in and the tops of the bed brought as near the glass as the flowers can mature without injury. Between the 1st and 15th of July sow the seed thinly in drills two inches deep and 18 inches apart. Water well after the bed has been made compact, and shade the glass until the plants are up and have made two inches of growth. They should then be thinned to twelve inches apart in the row. All the air possible should be given day and night, and as this is a season of the year in which moisture evaporates rapidly, the beds, even though they are solid, must be closely watched while the seed is germinating, and watered enough to prevent any dry spots from appearing. When the plants begin to push out their leaves, the shading should all be removed and pains taken to keep the glass clear. If butterflies appear, dust the plants with slug shot once or twice a week. It will not harm the plants and will effectually rid the house of the butterfly. As with chrysanthemums, if fine spikes of bloom are wanted, all laterals must be removed and the strength of the plant thrown into the flowering shoot. The house should be kept as cool as possible the first six weeks, and with the approach of cold weather a night temperature not to exceed 45° should be the standard. Should the thermometer fall to 40° occasionally, the effect will be to strengthen the bloom stems. All the air necessary to maintain a temperature of from 55° to 65° by day should be given.

As this plant is also subject to fungoid disease, it is well to adopt precautionary measures. As a rule, it will be found to be better to apply the water necessary to be used during winter to the soil direct, refraining from the use of cold water on the foliage as much as possible.

The particular form of fungus to which mignonette is liable, Prof. Seymour tells us, is very contagious, spreading from plant to plant with great rapidity. Its appearance is that of wilted or dried spots on the leaves, and oftentimes the whole leaf is destroyed by it.

Upon the first signs of its appearance, syringing should be resorted to, using the same formula as given for violets on page 195, and though it may not in all cases prevent its increase, it is as yet the best known agent in that direction.

CHAPTER XXXVII.

THE FORCING OF BULBS.

So many of our American growers are of foreign parentage, if not themselves born and reared where all that pertains to the care and culture of bulbous stock is very familiar, it may seem to them like a waste of space to treat of a subject so generally understood. It must be remembered that with the rapid development of this country, many men are led every year to take up our industry without having had enough special training for it. To such, this chapter will contain as much of interest, probably, as any that have preceded it, and if they are desirous of learning, it will be equally beneficial to them.

Whatever bulbs are used for this purpose, it will be to the interest of the grower to purchase none but the best. Narcissus, Roman hyacinths and tulips are available during August and September. It is much more convenient to plant these in boxes than in pots. The boxes should be made three inches deep and of a size to economize bench room in the house where they are to mature. Narcissus and white Romans should be planted about two inches apart, but tulips may be nearer together. In the northern states it is very convenient to have a cold house where they may be stored until the roots are well grown and the bulbs wanted for maturing their flowers. If this is not to be had, water well after planting, and place the boxes on well drained ground, arranging and labeling them so the kinds wanted for early flowering may be readily found. Cover the boxes with about three inches of soil, and as cold weather approaches give a covering that will exclude frost, as it is anything but pleasant work to take them out when frozen in one mass. Tulips and Romans will not be injured by light freezing, but narcissus are more tender and will not endure it. Of those mentioned Paper White narcissus are the earliest, and if planted in August they may be brought into flower in November. If a succession of flower is desired, bring in the number of boxes wanted every two weeks, planting and setting away others to take their places, but these should have four weeks at least in which to make root, before being placed in heat. Von Sion needs the same treatment, but no attempt should be made to bring it into flower before the middle or last of January. Both these and White Romans should be given an inside temperature of from 65° to 70°.

Tulips should all be planted when received and encouraged to make all the root growth they will. If planted early, those varieties which are the first to bloom can be brought inside soon after the middle of November and matured in a temperature of from 65° to 75°. In order to draw the stems, some growers place them over the pipes under the bench and curtain the front of the bench to exclude a portion of the light. Care must be taken in this case to give them plenty of water. Others grow on the benches in a temperature of 75° to 80°, and cover the under side of the glass with cheese cloth. This also tends to lengthen the stem.

The great thing to be assured of is, that all varieties are well rooted. This accomplished, succeeding steps are easy.

Freesias should be boxed every three or four weeks, allowed to root well in a cool room or pit, and brought in as wanted. They require about the same temperature as described for Narcissus, and can be brought to bloom in from 12 to 14 weeks after they are rooted.

Unlike the bulbs just described, lily of the valley cannot be obtained before November, and pips from the new crop can rarely be forced with satisfactory results for Christmas. For this reason a few large growers have built refrigerators in which to store them for use until wanted. Those stored in this way are used through the following fall and early winter, the new crop being used only for late winter and spring flowering.

When the lily of the valley arrives it should all be heeled away in sand or soil under some kind of a roof, so that rains shall not drench it. The sand in which the roots are packed should be moist, and about two inches should be placed between each row of bunches. When all are in or the frame is full, cover two inches deep with sand which is not as moist as that used for

THE FORCING OF BULBS. 201

the roots. This will protect the flower buds from the direct action of frosts, while the sand below will keep them plump.

For convenience, the bench in which they are forced should not be over two feet wide, and if enough are

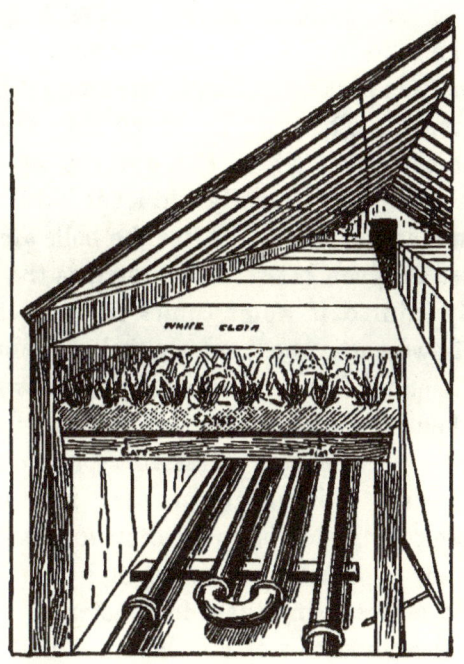

Fig. 40.

handled to be able to devote a house to them it can be arranged as seen in Fig. 40. The sides of the bench should be sealed up, doors being provided at the same time for the escape of heat when it is not all wanted beneath the bench. Cloth screens should also be hinged that may be either used on the under side of the glass, or as a cover for the beds as desired.

Before putting the pips in the forcing house, trim the roots so they will more readily absorb water. They need not be left more than two inches long. Plant them in the sand in rows, letting the rows be from two to three inches apart according to the amount of foliage they will make. The sand in which they are planted should indicate from 80° to 85°, and the top temperature 65°. Use water liberally and let it be of the same temperature as the house. After the bells are formed, water must be given between the rows, as the bloom is very easily injured if water comes in contact with it. Matured flowers may be kept several days by freshly cutting the ends of the stems, changing the water, and keeping them in a cool place.

The forcing of lilies has increased rapidly during the past few years. With some growers, near our large cities, these constitute the main crop for Easter. Mr. James Dean, an extensive grower of lilies, thus gives his method of preparing them for Easter:

"Fully three-quarters of all the lilies that are now forced are Harrisii, which is a great deal more profitable to grow, as it flowers more freely than the Longiflorum, and the plants are not liable to come blind. It can be forced with safety at a higher temperature than the Longiflorum, and if the plants are removed to a temperature of 50 degrees at night and given air during the day two weeks before the flowers open, they will be just as firm as the Longiflorum and you will be able to cut nearly double the number of flowers. Most of the lily bulbs come from Bermuda, arriving here during the months of July and August. On the receipt of the bulbs they are potted in a light, sandy loam to which has been added about one-third of well rotted manure, using a $5\frac{1}{2}$ and 6 inch pot for the 5 to 7 inch bulbs; a $6\frac{1}{2}$ and 7 inch pot for the 7 to 9 inch bulbs; and a 7 and 8 inch pot for the 9 to 12 inch bulbs. In potting the bulb we place it about one inch below the surface of soil. They are then set close together in a frame out of doors, given a good watering and covered with a mulch of hay or straw which prevents the soil from drying out so rapidly and saves watering. They can remain out of doors until frost comes, although a degree or two of frost will not injure the plants. From the time they are brought into the greenhouse until New Years, a night temperature of 40° to 45° with plenty of air during the day is all they require. After New Years they may be removed to another house or the night temperature increased to 60° or 65° and even to 70° if the weather proves bad and there is little sunshine. Try to have the flower buds well above the foliage six weeks before Easter, so that standing in the door way of the greenhouse you can plainly see all the buds; bearing constantly in mind that it is a great deal easier to hold the flowers back by shading and giving plenty of air, which hardens and stiffens them and enables them to bear transportation better, than when you are compelled to hurry them into flower by steaming the pipes, and watering them with warm water. Under such treatment they are fit only for the rubbish heap."

When lilies are wanted for earlier bloom, they may be brought inside whenever they are well rooted in the pots. They should be given a temperature of 50° for the first few days, gradually increasing it to 65° or 70°, lowering it again for a week to 55° after the flowers are matured in order to harden them. From 10 to 12 weeks will be required from the time they are brought into heat before they will be in bloom.

The greatest enemy of the lily is green fly, and these must be kept at bay from the first.

Lilium candidum is but little grown of late years, but is still called for to some extent for use in work wherever smaller flowers than Harrisii are wanted. As these bulbs loose in vitality rapidly by exposure to the air, it is better to use home grown bulbs, or if imported ones are received, to plant them for a year. As soon as their flowering season outside is over, lift such as are wanted, putting two in a 7 or 8 inch pot, using a light soil for potting them. Plunge these pots to the rim and leave outside until early in November, when they may be brought into a temperature of 50°, gradually raising it to 60°, and flowers may in this way be obtained in from 12 to 14 weeks. Give plenty of water during the period of growth, adding liquid manure as they seem to need it.

The calla lily is a bulb that needs rest, and it will give more flowers when grown in pots. Planted on benches it is inclined to make too much foliage. After the flowering season is past, or as early as the first of July, take them to the shade of some building and lay the pots on their side for the first week, giving them a light sprinkling once a day. After this, turn the pots every other day for two weeks. By the middle of August they should be shaken out, trimmed, repotted, watered well and plunged in a partially shaded place. Give them one shift, letting the size of the pot be proportioned to the size and age of the bulb, and bring them into the house before there is any danger of frost.

From the time the pots are filled with roots, they should never be allowed to become dry. Place the pots in saucers and see that these are always supplied with water. Ammonia used in the water is beneficial to them, also weak liquid manure. If it is desired to mature a crop of blooms quickly, it may be accomplished by giving them water each day for a short time as hot as can be borne by the hand. Water that is applied directly to the roots, should always be warmer than the temperature of the house. This should not be less than 65°.

CHAPTER XXXVIII.
ORCHIDS.

So much might be written on this subject I hesitate to commence, lest no stopping place be found before the limited amount of space that can be accorded to it in these pages shall be exhausted. Orchids fill so large a place in the world of flowers to-day, and have come to be so much of a necessity in some localities—notably those occupied by people of wealth—that our list of winter cut flowers would seem incomplete without some mention of them. We will therefore consider them very briefly and with reference to the wants of the retail grower and amateur rather than to those of the wholesaler. For extensive commercial growing, perhaps more than any other family do these need to be made a specialty.

To be grown on a large scale, requires first, a large capital. Second, it is necessary that a person should have received a practical training in all that pertains to their cultivation. The demand for this class of flowers is of such recent date many growers who are expert in the cultivation of other kinds of plants, would find themselves somewhat at sea were they to undertake the culture of Orchids on a scale at par with the lines they are already accustomed to. Again, from the very nature of things, the price of these flowers must be high for years to come, and as a consequence will be beyond the reach of many who buy liberally of other kinds.

Specialists in this line who already have large stocks of plants from which to produce the flowers, will probably be able to meet transient demands for sometime to come.

To the retailer, however, who grows a part or all of his own flowers, there exists a necessity for being able to supply the wants of his customers if he would keep pace with his competitors in business. To accomplish this in the best way is the object we have under consideration.

If you have a home trade, and it is of a nature that demands a good line of decorative plants, you can grow a few Orchids with both pleasure and profit to yourself, as well as pleasure, if not profit, to your customers. It may take a little time to educate people to their use, but you will find it to be a great advertising medium, and if the public is invited on some special day to inspect your display which has been carefully arranged for the purpose, you will undoubtedly find that you will be more than compensated in other ways even if no sales of Orchids are made at first.

The varieties of Orchids profitable to the retail grower thrive well in the same temperature, shade and moisture as are given to palms, and decorative plants of like nature. They may also be suspended or hung upon posts in various places in the house that would not otherwise be occupied. Thus the cost of housing practically amounts to very little.

Open wooden baskets for growing them, or pots made for the purpose, are preferable to charred wood or wooden blocks. Fill the basket with fern roots and live sphagnum moss, after providing an abundance of broken crockery and charcoal for drainage. Fasten the plant securely to the top of the basket or pot with wire and assign it to its place in the house.

Cypripedium insigne is one of the most common Orchids in cultivation, and of exceedingly easy culture; it commences to bloom in November and continues until March.

Of the many *Cattleyas*, *Percivilliana* is the earliest, commencing to bloom in the fall and continuing nearly to Christmas. This is followed by *C. Trianæ*, which should be in flower during the period cut flowers are most in demand, from January to April.

C. Mossiæ blooms through the spring until the appearance of warm weather.

With these four varieties a succession of flowers may be obtained extending through the months during which the sale of cut flowers is most profitable.

This small list is the most suitable for a beginner, be he florist or amateur. Other varieties can be added from time to time as desired, but those mentioned will will be found to give a succession of bloom, and should constitute the bulk of a stock kept for flowering.

In watering, the same principle should be observed with Orchids as with other plants. During the period of rest, which commences after the growth is completed, and the new flowering bulb has been formed, water should be withheld from them, the moisture existing in a palm-house being sufficient to keep them in good condition. Let them have only as much water as is needed to keep the bulbs plump, increasing the amount with their growth, and providing an abundance when the roots are most active.

CHAPTER XXXIX.

MISCELLANEOUS TOPICS.

CLEANLINESS.

Some one has called the Carnation the "Divine Flower." Not only this, but all flowers reflect the love of the Divine for man, and for this reason, if no other, their claim to cleanly surroundings is supreme. But this is not the only reason, for both beauty and purity are much enhanced by the exercise of this great virtue, increasing the pleasures which form and fragrance bring to our senses, as well as the corresponding value arising from more perfect conditions of growth.

The first step in this direction should be taken when the crop in any house is to be renewed. After removing the old soil and repairing such parts of the benching as may need it, go over the whole ground surface, sweeping thoroughly and removing any scattered soil or other accumulations, after which thoroughly scald the house. No place of any size can be considered complete without having a boiler for this purpose, no matter what the system of heating may be. Usually this boiler can be used for other purposes also,—power, tempering of water, or for steam circulation. The interest on two or three hundred dollars bears no comparison to the benefit derived, even if the boiler is used for this sole purpose and remains idle ten months of the year. The boiler once set can be attached to the water system, thus requiring but little expense in extra pipe, and this connection should be made with the "blow-off" at the rear. When a house is ready for scalding fill the boiler four-fifths full of water, heat it thoroughly, and when from forty to fifty pounds pressure is indicated on the steam gauge, draw the fire. Connect a hose with the hydrant to be used. Fasten to the end of this a "leader" in much the same way you would a ring in the nose of an animal. Take the "leader" in one hand and with a thick glove the hose in the other, open the connecting valves and the head of steam will drive all the water from the boiler. With this, thoroughly scald every inch of ground surface, the benches, walls and sides of gutters. By opening the ends of the building before commencing, a draft will be created which will obviate any inconvenience arising from the hot steam, care being taken, of course, to begin at the end at which the draft escapes from the house. Never attempt this without a "leader" with which to guide the stream of boiling water as the pressure drives it through the hose. You might as well dance around among the folds of a living snake, or attempt to lead a refractory animal with a string. Do not ever commence, either, until the fire has been drawn from the boiler, or ruin to it will be the result. The under sides of benches sometimes harbor vermin and are hard to reach in all parts with the stream of hot water. To make thorough work, shut the house up tight, and burn sulphur under them. This can be done by means of the stoves spoken of for fumigating, or if you do not have these, red hot bricks will answer the purpose. The only care to be taken is not to have plants within reach of the sulphur fumes. Salt is very cheap, and a liberal coat of it applied after this on the ground under the benches will not only prevent weeds from springing up, but will render it almost impossible for insects to burrow and live in the soil. After this has been done, whitewash all interior surfaces of benches and walls. Wash, if needed, and paint all roof and gutter work, and you are prepared to commence anew. This process, followed every year, is almost equal in results to those experienced with new houses, which old growers will tell you increase the probabilities of success by a large per cent. These conditions of cleanliness should be maintained as far as practicable throughout the season. All litter, dirt and dead leaves, as well as weeds both on and under the benches should be persistently removed. It is well to have a box in some convenient corner at each end of the house, in which may be placed from day to day rejected blooms, leaves and buds resulting from succoring or disbudding, instead of allowing them to be thrown on the ground or behind the benches. Have the walks swept as often as necessary, and it will be found that when these are constructed with cement and the centre raised just enough to turn the water, it will greatly facilitate the object sought.

POT RACKS.

In this same connection, nothing helps to litter a house more than the storing of pots under the benches, the dirt and breakage attending their constant removal back and forth being very great, nor is it a sign of thrift

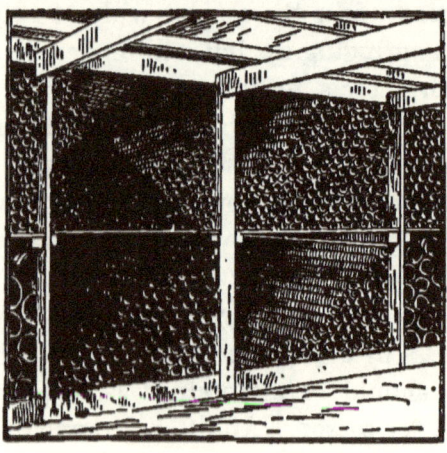

Fig. 41.

to see houses so incumbered. Every place, no matter how small it is, should have provision made for unused pots in some locality convenient to the potting bench, where all the sizes may be kept by themselves and be ready at hand when wanted for use. The waste from breakage is less, and much more time is saved each season than would build a convenient pot rack every year. (See Fig. 41.)

PREPARATION OF SOIL.

In this, several things are sought to be accomplished. The decomposition, as well as the preservation of the fibre, destruction of, and protection against insect enemies, and the thorough mingling of all ingredients added to the soil.

At first thought there is a seeming inconsistency in the first two, both destruction and preservation being sought in the same thing. This is because time is required to turn the sod and make it tender, but it should not be so thoroughly decomposed as to destroy the fibre and thus allow the soil to pack too closely. All rose soil should contain sod and its roots. If it is a tough old blue grass sod, so much the better. The depth at which it should be taken must be regulated somewhat by the time elapsing before needed for use, as well as by the amount of land available. The ideal soil pile is composed of sods cut two inches deep and allowed to remain in the pile several months before being used. It should also be frozen in all sections possible to do it, in order to destroy worms and insects usually found in grass lands. Some recommend cutting and storing in seasons of extreme drought, claiming that in this condition no insect life will be found to exist. This I have never proved, but can recommend early winter frosts. If the sod is tough it can be so plowed as to stand partially on edge, and in this condition the first cold spell will freeze it thoroughly, after which it can be brought together in a pile, whatever is to be mixed with it added, and the whole be ready for turning early in the spring. This cannot always be accomplished in this way even in frosty sections, but some means should be devised for its accomplishment, and if no other offers, the labor entailed in the plan outlined on page 105 is to be preferred to using soil that has not been thus renovated. There are but few roses that will not be benefited by an addition to the soil of at least one-fifth manure—some use as much as one-third. In either case, especially in that of the larger amount, it must have been so well composted when added to the soil, as to have nearly disappeared when the soil is ready for use, or to have become so thoroughly incorporated as to be nearly indistinguishable. If green manure is all that can be had, not more than one yard, to seven of sod should be used, in which case more dependence will have to be had on the various modes of top dressing as the plants require it. Whatever manure is used, it should be applied in layers as the pile is formed, and when turned, the pile should be cut through in narrow strips from top to bottom and well mixed. Piles put up late in the fall will require early and close attention in order to have them in readiness for the first planting. If more time elapses, turning need not be as frequent. In case sufficient fibre is not present in the soil when gathered, layers of straw through the pile and incorporated with it will be of benefit, though it will not take the place of good grass sod.

FERTILIZERS.

For mixing with the soil, nothing equals grain fed cow manure. Avoid distillery products as you would poison, for slops from these stalls are as fatal to plant life as is the so-called refined product to man. The writer has proved both and knows whereof he speaks. Keep at least two years stock of manure on hand—three if you can. This should always be kept under cover, as exposure to storms greatly lessens its value. To prevent the May beetle from depositing her eggs, from which the white grub is hatched, turn the compost piles in April, smooth down the surface and cover two inches deep with plain soil, or that in which there is no manure, and she will seek a more congenial atmosphere elsewhere. Of commercial fertilizers, none are so valuable for all crops as pure flour of bone, *but be sure it is pure.* Some years since the writer lost $2,000 worth of new roses through the use of bone which had been cut with acids. The manufacturer's purse being the longer, discretion counseled bearing the loss in silence, which was done. This experience leads me to emphasize the advice given, that you know absolutely that the article you are using is pure. With a change of manufacturers I have since found no trouble, and have used it freely every season. This is a matter of so much importance to all growers that I cannot do less than to say the article last referred to is obtained of the Cincinnati Dessicating Co. For field carnations unleached ashes sown broadcast and worked into the soil are very beneficial, they are also good as a top dressing on benches when used in small quantities. It will be remembered the color of Toronto grown Woottons was referred to in the cultural notes on that variety. Since those notes were written, I have been told by one in whom I have every confidence, and who is in a position to know, that the extraordinary size and color produced by our Canadian growers in this particular variety was the result of a liberal use of unleached hard wood ashes. No opportunity has been had to test this personally since learning of it, and I would say to those disposed to try it, do so carefully until it proves to do for you as it is claimed to do for others. That ashes are good for almost any field crop is a well known fact, but without having given them any very practical test on the rose, I had formed the opinion there were other fertilizers that were better. Nitrate of soda has already been referred to, and it only remains to say in addition, if used at all, let it be with the greatest care. Only a few days since, in visiting a florist in another city, I was surprised to see the condition of his roses, as he has the reputation of being a good grower. Enquiring the reason, he told me it was through the use of the article in question. Careful man as he is, he had, unwittingly, used enough to burn the surface roots. Action was destroyed, water had to be withheld, and the plants allowed to go dormant for a time, and this during the three months when flowers are in the greatest demand. While exceedingly sorry for his loss, many of us have been in the same position, not from just such a cause, perhaps, but through over-confidence in what we were trying, either as an experiment of our own, or acting on the advice of others. Another argument for conducting experiments on a small scale.

The application of aqua ammonia to the roots of plants, has also been referred to. For roses it is sometimes beneficial when used on the foliage, but I would not advise it, unless from some cause they need a quick stimulant late in the season, and then only on plants that are to be rejected at its close. No doubt many of these more powerful liquids stimulate a plant to greater exertion for a short time, but as a rule it is safer to confine stimulants to such as seem to be the natural food of all plants. If your soil has been properly prepared they will find in it all the food they can assimilate for the first two months. When the last mulching seems exhausted, liquids may be applied with beneficial results if abundant root action is present to absorb it, but it should not be given too strong, or when the soil is dry. If it is found desirable to use liquid food to any extent, use it lightly once or twice a week as the state of the soil demands, and change the ingredients from time to time. A peck of fresh cow manure after remaining twenty-four hours in a barrel of water will be as strong as should be used. Alternate with the same quantity of sheep manure prepared in the same way, and that with half the quantity from the poultry yard. This in turn may be changed for one-half pint of aqua ammonia in a barrel of water, after which commence with the first if more is needed. Liquids should never be applied to a dry soil. If the bed has for any reason become dry, or dry in spots, go over it first with clear water giving the larger portion of what is needed in this way, following with the liquid to be applied. Experience and watchfulness alone can regulate the amount and frequency of the applications.

Horn shavings are used by some, both in the soil and by letting them stand in water a few days and then using the liquid. I also know of some who will not use them the second time, having had all the ex-

FERTILIZERS.

perience they desire in that line already. While some have used them successfully, they are dangerous and should be avoided.

Beware of trying new things on a large scale, before proving them for yourself. This has not reference so much to plants as to methods of building, food given to plants, or any treatment not in accord with past experience or good common sense. Experimenting is one of the ways by which we learn, but it should be conducted on a small scale until proved to be both useful and reliable. The instance recently cited of the loss that attended the use of nitrate of soda, is only one of the many where great loss has occurred through using certain things largely on the recommendation of others. $5,000 would not compensate the man of my acquaintance who risked his crop in the season of '92 on horn shavings. Opportunities for success coming with each year, if lost, never come again; a whole year's work is blotted out. Worse than that, there is danger that the savings of years of toil may go with it. Some years ago an acquaintance conceived the idea that his hot water pipes needed a preservative, so during the early fall he gave them a coat of coal tar. A more senseless thing was never thought of, and still we occasionally hear of a case of this kind, and they are always attended with the same results, a total loss of the crop for the season. It is to be hoped the next generation will be wiser.

A more recent error—for mistake I believe it to be—is the use of soil for any purpose but field work, that has been used in the houses one season. Rejected rose soil is rich in unspent food, and will bear abundant crops in the field where it can be fully exposed to sunshine and air, but I have never seen good results from its use for any crop the second year, indoors. When used for potting, as it sometimes is, instead of great white feeding roots being thrown out, they are often small and wiry, and plants are not apt to flourish in it. As I write the case of two growers comes to my mind who are lamenting the fact that they persuaded themselves the past season to plant their carnations in spent rose soil, an experiment they will not try again, as it has lessened the production by at least one-third. Considerable has been written in relation to this matter of late by growers having a soil composed largely of mica. This soil seems to be well adapted to the growth of the carnation, cultivators telling us but little manure can be used with it, and while those in possession of soil of this nature may be able to use the same more than one year, the rule does not hold good with soils that must be heavily fertilized. The writer dried out a pile of rejected rose soil the past season, thinking thus to sweeten and counteract any sourness there might be in it, and used it for carnations. The result is not satisfactory, leading to the conclusion that the best is none too good for artificial growth. For all flowering plants use nothing but new, fresh, sweet soil. Make it rich with all the food the plants will assimilate, but let the basis of it each and every year, be virgin sod fresh from the field.

CRUDE OIL.

The use of this as a preservative is advocated by many, while others are emphatic and decided in their belief that it is injurious. The writer once washed with it some new boards used in a partition wall. The bench near them was afterwards planted to Duchess of Albany, time enough having elapsed for the oil to become perfectly dry and all scent to evaporate. The result was, these plants rusted badly, while others, from the same lot, planted on another bench, in the same kind of soil, all the conditions in fact being the same save in the use of the oil, remained perfectly healthy. No form of plant life seems to have any affinity for this product when brought in contact with it in any quantity, and it seems reasonable to suppose small quantities are proportionately injurious, though it may scarcely be perceptible. I would much rather chance a bed covered with decomposed hops than coal oil, whether for the growth of carnations or roses, and even if the result required a renewal of the lumber one-third sooner in the former case, I believe that the increased product would more than compensate for its early decay. It is best to keep on the safe side of all things about which cultivators disagree. We oftentimes see roots growing in the decayed tissues of the bench when the soil is removed, but I do not believe that any one ever saw the same where the bench had been washed with crude oil the fall before. Lime we know is a preservative in a small degree, besides being food for plants. If any part of a building is benefited by the use of oil without injury to a crop, it is the posts which form the walls, but an exterior coat is claimed by some to be injurious to the timber if applied while the sap is present in the wood. If the posts are seasoned and placed in a vat and the pores allowed to fill with the oil, there can be little doubt but what the life of the timber is greatly lengthened.

Another preservative of wood is cement, some claiming the life of a bench is twice as long when washed with this yearly. However this may be, from the nature of the material it seems safe, and is to be commended on that account, if it is desired to use anything but lime for this purpose.

RESTORING LOST VITALITY TO ROSES.

In relation to the necessity of this, opinions vary, some claiming that a ceaseless round of propagation and growth of our tea roses will, in the end, produce this result. The writer has never experienced any necessity for taking rested stock for this purpose. As usually advocated, it is a very expensive method to follow, requiring for its accomplishment two seasons of growth. The vitality of a tea rose is often impaired through the ignorance or neglect of conditions pertaining to a healthy growth, and when the plant sickens, or ceases to be profitable as a producer, it is easy to see that its vitality is impaired, but the cause is sometimes misstated, and should be laid at the door of the operator, instead of to the constitution of the plant.

I have now in process of construction a block of houses for summer growing exclusively. In these such of the winter flowering varieties as will thrive in a summer temperature will be planted, and from the dormant wood of these, after the term of flowering is over in the fall, a series of experiments will be made in order to fully test the advantage, if any, that is to be derived from a partial rest. Any grower who has stock in a condition to try this method, can easily satisfy himself as to its utility, without the risk of loss or expense. The cuttings should be treated much as are those of hard wood, rooted slowly in a cool house, but after once rooted no check should ever be permitted to occur in their growth.

DISBUDDING ROSES.

During the summer it is better to let no buds mature, but the practice of nipping them out as soon as they appear is to be deprecated, as it leaves a mass of eyes on unripe wood, and these tend to augment the habit some varieties have of throwing blind wood. The better way is to let the bud partially mature or remain until its supporting stem has attained firmness and strength, then cut back one-third or one-half its length, as deemed advisable, or to a good strong eye, which in turn will quickly break and produce another strong bud-producing shoot. The strongest of the blind wood should be allowed to remain to feed the plant, until such time as its usefulness in this respect is passed, but the weak, spindling wood of this class should be removed after the plants have attained some size. This practice of disbudding should cease with the advent of cool weather, or whenever the market demands the product and the plants are strong enough to mature them without injury, but in most varieties the laterals should be removed in order to throw all the strength of the plant to the maturing bud.

THE CARE OF BOILERS.

Too much stress cannot be laid upon a careful annual inspection of so important a factor to success as is our heating apparatus. In relation to its care, when not in use, I do not think a better method can be recommended than that given a few years since in answer to this same question: The proper care of our boilers is a very important matter, as they bear in a measure much the same relation to our business as do the foundations of a building to the superstructure. Let these be faulty and trouble arises. Let our boilers fail at a critical time and disaster and loss are sure to follow.

But I find an answer to the question, as to what is the best treatment to accord them during their period of rest, a difficult one to give; for like many others it is one on which doctors disagree.

I have interviewed several parties, persons prominent either in the erection or care of these structures and find each has a theory or practice of his own. Doubtless we all have our views upon the best methods, as well as our own ways of caring for our boilers, but I am afraid that in the majority of instances they are left to care for themselves. A. tells me to empty the boilers and let them stand dry—good advice if they can be kept so; B. says keep them full; while C. tells me to empty, take off the doors, take out the grates, carefully remove all ashes adhering to the fire-box, and see that there is a free circulation of air through the flues all the time. There are good points in each of these methods, but it must be remembered that in four cases out of five,—and I might safely say, I think, nine out of ten,—boilers are in situations damp of themselves, and this dampness is largely increased by every rainfall, causing a continual corrosion of the exposed surface. My own way would be this: Leave the boilers full of water, carefully remove from and about them everything of a nature to retain moisture, thoroughly cleanse the flues, remove as far as possible all rust or scale from the flue sheets and from all the iron accessible, and then give the whole inside surface a thorough dressing with crude or linseed oil. For an outside dressing, paint with asphaltum that has been cut with turpentine. Stop all draft so as to prevent damp air from circulating through the flues. Lastly, if your boilers are old, have them carefully inspected by a competent person, if you cannot do it yourself, as soon in the spring as they can be spared, in order that they may be in thorough repair for early fall work.

MORTAR FOR FIRE BRICK.

While conducting a series of experiments with clay some years since, I discovered that a mixture of common clay and crude oil would endure great heat, and continue to harden under its influence. For the inside lining of walls, or fire boxes that are constructed of fire brick, if the brick are laid in this mortar, the joints will be nearly as durable as the brick themselves.

To make the mortar, the clay should be dry. Pulverize it fine, and mix it with enough crude petroleum oil to bring it to the state of pliability desired, kneading and mixing it thoroughly. Use no more between the joints than is necessary to set the brick firmly. The interior of a fire box may also be temporarily repaired with this mortar, when burned out in places, by filling the vacancies with it. This will oftentimes save the rebuilding of the wall until such time as it can be conveniently performed.

TO STOP A LEAK.

Leaks in heating pipes sometimes occur at a time when fires cannot be dispensed with long enough to repair them permanently. If these leaks are found to be caused by a flaw in the pipe, or by an opening seam, they can be controlled temporarily in the following manner: Mix fine sand with white lead until it is of the consistency of putty; spread this half an inch thick on a strip of canvas, long and wide enough to cover the rent; if possible shut off the pressure of steam, or flow of water; apply the cement and canvas to the pipe, and bind it securely with a canvas bandage. When this is accomplished take some strong cord, commence at one end winding tight and close, until the whole surface is firmly covered with the cord. Great damage can often be prevented in this way, especially when cast iron pipe fails at a season of the year at which permanent repairs are impossible.

Should a seam open in a steam pipe which is required to resist several pounds of pressure, and at a time when permanent repairs cannot be made, split a piece of rubber hose and lay it over the seam. Cover this with a semi-circular piece of iron that will fit the pipe closely. Fasten all to the pipe by means of clamps similar to those used to fasten wood work to the axletree of a buggy. If one is living at a distance from where these materials can be quickly obtained, it will be prudent to have a few on hand before the commencement of cold weather.

The following advertisements have the endorsement of the author of this book. First, because he has had occasion to prove their worth in his own business. Second, because a personal acquaintance with the men and firms they represent, has satisfied him they are men worthy of the confidence of all tradesmen.

GUARANTEED

.. PURE ..
BONE
FLOUR

Manufactured with great care
for the special use of

ROSE GROWERS
AND
GREENHOUSE MEN

POSITIVELY FREE FROM SULPHURIC ACID.

Prices and samples furnished
on application to

CINCINNATI DESICCATING CO.
No. 851 West Sixth St.   CINCINNATI, OHIO.

Greenhouse Construction Lumber.

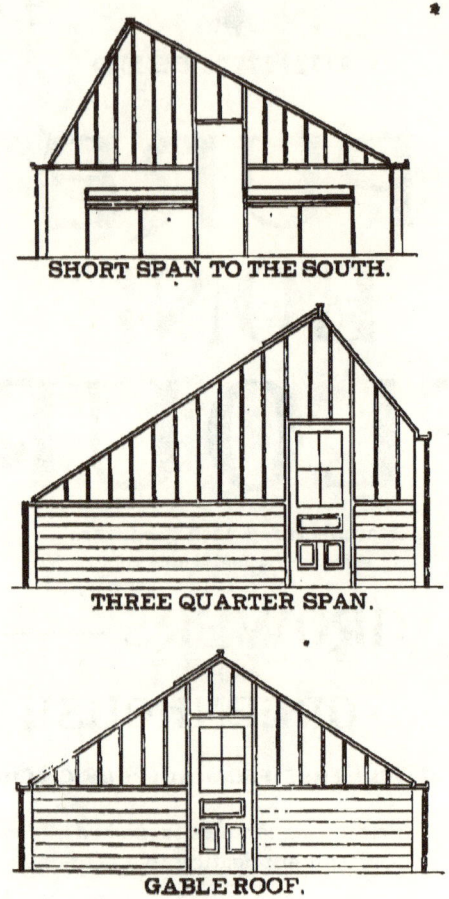

SHORT SPAN TO THE SOUTH.

THREE QUARTER SPAN.

GABLE ROOF.

See opposite page.

John C. Moninger,

SUCCESSOR TO JOHN L. DIEZ & CO.

MANUFACTURER OF

Cypress Building Material,

—FOR—

Greenhouses, Rosehouses and Conservatories.

OFFICE AND FACTORY,
297 TO 307 HAWTHORN AVE.

CHICAGO, ILLINOIS

Catalogue on Application.

THE FAULTLESS FURMAN
STEAM AND HOT WATER
BOILERS
For GREENHOUSE HEATING.

Used in the Green- houses of the Principal Agricul- tural Colleges

Used in Heating the World's Fair Green- houses.

ECONOMICAL, SUBSTANTIAL, SAFE.
SCREW JOINTS

Hence no leakage. Vertical Circulation; rapid flow. Cool Smoke Pipe; Economy in Fuel. Large Fire Box; requires very little attention.

Send for Our Large Catalogue and Book on "Modern Green- house Heating"—FREE.

HERENDEEN MF'G CO.
10 Fay St., GENEVA, N. Y.

The Evans Improved Challenge Roller Bearing Ventilating Apparatus.

This the Best! Why?

No pull on the roof. No friction on the pipe. Self acting. Operates quicker and easier. A child can operate a 100 foot house. The only roller bearing ventilating apparatus on the market. Roller bearing is to a ventilating apparatus as ball bearing is to a bicycle. Illustrated catalogue free. Address,

QUAKER CITY MACHINE CO.

Richmond, Indiana.

KEEP YOUR  ON US.

EVERY WIDE-AWAKE, PROGRESSIVE

 **FLORIST**

WHEN NEEDING

**CUT FLOWERS,
FLOWER SEEDS,
FALL BULBS,
SPRING BULBS,
OR FLORISTS' SUPPLIES**

OF ANY KIND WHATEVER TURNS FIRST TO

HUNT

As it is well known he keeps NEARLY EVERYTHING the trade requires.

E. H. HUNT, SEEDSMAN,

79 Lake Street.   **CHICAGO, ILL.**

☞ SEND FOR CATALOGUE.

The .... John Davis Company,

69 to 79 Michigan Street,
CHICAGO.

CONTRACTORS FOR

GREEN= HOUSE HEATING APPARATUS

AND DEALERS IN

———All Kinds of Material———

FOR

GREEN=HOUSE =:= HEATING.

Write for Prices.

ESTABLISHED 1854.   INCORPORATED 1892.

FRANK DAN. BLISH, President.
WELLS B. SIZER, Vice-President.
DANIEL W. BLISH, Secretary.
ARTHUR HATFIELD, Treasurer.

DEVINE BOILER WORKS,
Steam and Hot Water Boilers

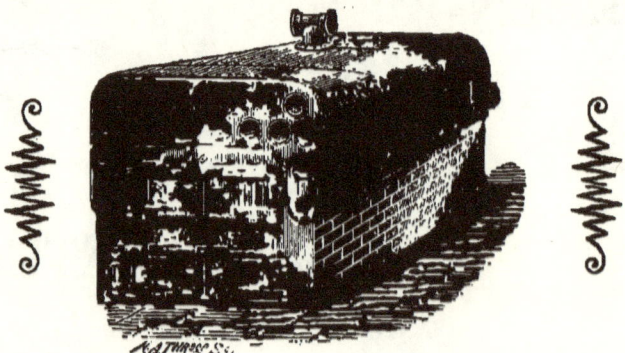

SCHILLER No. 9 HOT WATER BOILER,

As used in Greenhouses of M. A. Hunt and many others. Photographs on receipt of inquiry.

Shops, Fifty-Sixth and Wallace Sts.

OFFICE, 189 STATE ST., CHICAGO, U. S. A.

ROSE·LEAF
Extract of Tobacco.

SURE DEATH .. to all Insects infesting Greenhouses, and a certain cure for the diseases caused by Parasite Life to ...

FLOWERS, VEGETABLES AND PLANTS.
Also an Excellent FERTILIZER.

For Particulars as to its use, see Page 116, this Book.

Packed in 5 Gallon Cans.
Price $1.50 per gallon, F. O. B.

MANUFACTURED BY
LOUISVILLE SPIRIT CURED TOBACCO CO.
LOUISVILLE, KY., U. S. A.

Moore and Langen ...

22
24
26 South Fifth Street.

TERRE HAUTE, IND.

Printers

Book Binders

Blank Book Makers

Floral Catalogues a Specialty.

www.ingramcontent.com/pod-product-compliance
Lightning Source LLC
Chambersburg PA
CBHW021359230426
43666CB00006B/575